DISCOVERING JESUS

ALSO BY WILLIAM BARCLAY IN THIS SERIES

Discovering Jesus

WILLIAM BARCLAY

Westminster John Knox Press
Louisville, Kentucky

Published in the U.S.A. in 2000 by
Westminster John Knox Press
Louisville, Kentucky

Printed in Singapore

00 01 02 03 04 05 06 07 08 09 – 10 9 8 7 6 5 4 3 2 1

A catalog card for this book may be obtained from the Library of Congress

ISBN 0-664-22192-0

CONTENTS

Preface

The form of these chapters has been decided by the purpose for which they were first produced. The chapters consist of six talks on the Life of Jesus given on Scottish BBC Television in Lent 1965. The chapters have been kept in almost exactly the spoken form in which they were delivered. Had they originally been written in order to be read, their form might have been very different; but they were written to be listened to, and I have thought it better to leave them as they are.

The pattern of these chapters has again been decided by the purpose for which they were produced. The aim here was not to study in detail but to try to see on a large scale the whole panorama of the unfolding drama of the life of Jesus. Preparation, Conflict, Recognition, Tragedy, Triumph, the continuing life of Jesus in his Church - these are the main themes and the acts in the drama. My whole intention has been, not to study in depth, but to see the drama as a whole. And all the time my intention was to speak, not to the scholar and the theologian, not even to those within the Church to whom the story is familiar, but rather to speak to the ordinary man and woman.

Trinity College
WILLIAM BARCLAY
Glasgow

Editor's Note

William Barclay might be called the people's theologian. As Le Lumealy is at pains to point out, he is communicating to 'the man in the street.' He is clear and simple and his style belies an effective method of reaching deep into profound understanding of Scripture and turning it out for popular readership. Indeed, his wish that people might 'see' Jesus in his words, does come true. 'If you are in Christ it means Christ is the atmosphere in which you live - you never forget the presence of Jesus Christ - you always remember he is with you.' For Barclay, this is the sense in which Christians are different - they are a New People!

1

PREPARATION

BC - before Christ. AD - in the year of our Lord. Even the calendar tells us that with the birth of Jesus Christ history started all over again. If a man's birth is the hinge of history, then it is certainly worth while trying to find out something about this man.

There are two ways of looking at anything. You can look at it with a microscope: and if you look at it with a microscope you see a very small part of it, and you see that very small part in the very greatest detail. Or you can look at it with a telescope, and if you look at it with a telescope you see the whole dramatic panorama and the whole pattern stretched out before you. Normally we look at the life of Jesus with the microscope; we take one incident, one verse, even one word, and we turn the microscope on that and we see it in the greatest possible detail. We have always got to go on doing that, for obviously every word that Jesus spoke is of the greatest possible importance to us. But there is a case every now and again for dropping the microscope and for taking up the telescope, and for looking at the life of Jesus to see its broad dramatic pattern. When you use the microscope you are very apt not to see the wood for the trees, and once in a while it is worth trying to see the dramatic story unfolding its broad lines before us.

Once Aristotle said that every play has a beginning, a middle and an end, and we are going to try to see the life of Jesus in these terms - Preparation, Conflict, Recognition, Tragedy and Triumph. Now whenever we try to do this we are up against a problem straight away. Jesus died when he was thirty-three, and of the first thirty years of his life we know next to nothing. We know one incident from his boyhood, an incident of first-rate importance as we are going to see, and we know one or two things which happened to him when he was a baby, but otherwise we know nothing at all. And it is a very difficult thing to try to write the biography of a man when you know practically nothing of ten-elevenths of his life. So how can we proceed? Well, although we don't know in detail what was happening to him in these early years of his life - although these are, as they are so often called, the hidden years - the fact remains that we can work out a good deal of what must have been happening to Jesus in these years of preparation.

The School and the World

First of all, there was the preparation of studying and of learning. When Jesus was a boy he went to the village school in Nazareth. A village teacher in Nazareth taught the boy who was going to have more impact on history than any other person ever had. We shall never know that teacher's name, but there was a teacher, who taught the boy who was also the Son of God. When you are a teacher you never know what you are doing!

In those days at school, of course, they had not got any books because printing had not yet been invented. Everything had to be hand-written on rolls. The rolls were tremendously expensive, and practically nobody could possess one for his own. Therefore if you were going to learn anything you had to learn it by heart. A Jewish boy when he went to school had to learn five things by heart.

First of all he had to learn the *Shema*, the basic creed of Judaism with which every synagogue service starts. *Shema* is the imperative of the Hebrew verb which means 'to hear'; it is the first word of the text: 'Hear, O Israel, the Lord thy God is one Lord and thou shalt love the Lord with all thy heart, with all thy soul, and with all thy strength.'

Secondly he would learn the *Hallel*, which means literally the 'Praise God'. The *Hallel* is Psalms 113–118, which are full of praise of God.

Thirdly he would learn Genesis 1–5, the story of creation and of how the world and the nations came into being.

Fourthly he would learn Leviticus 1–8. Leviticus is the law which tells of what is clean or unclean; what may be eaten and what may not be eaten; what may be touched and what may not be touched; and how a man can live a clean life according to the eyes of the Jewish law.

Scrolls of parchment - used for handwriting - that pre-dated printing

Fifthly the Jewish boy would be set to do something very interesting indeed. Although he had no books of his own, there were rolls and scrolls in the school, and he would be allowed to use these and to borrow them, and he was set searching for what was called a personal text. Now a personal text was a text which began with the first letter of his name and ended with the last letter of his name, and had all the other letters of his name included in between. For instance a text like this: 'A soft answer turns away wrath, but a grievous word stirs up anger', is a text for a boy called Abner, because it starts with 'A' and ends with 'R' and it has got B-N-E included in it.

The Jewish teacher sometimes gave his class a very interesting reward, which may have come to Jesus. In those days they had no paper and pencils, and they largely used slates and slate pencils or chalk, but

9

Map showing location of Nazareth and the Mediterranean, gateway to the rest of the world

sometimes the teacher would write the alphabet and he would write a sentence on a slate in a mixture of honey and flour; then he would take the slate and he would show it to a boy and say, 'What's that letter?' If the boy told him correctly, he was allowed to lick the letter off the slate. This is what the psalmist is referring to when he says, 'Thy words are sweeter to me than honey, and honey from the comb'.

So Jesus had the preparation of learning and the preparation of education in the school. But Jesus also had the preparation of an opening world. Now most people think that Palestine was just a little unimportant backwater on the way to nowhere. It certainly is true that Palestine was a very small country - from the north to the south the whole distance is just 126 miles. From east to west, Palestine was 46 miles. (It is further from Glasgow to Edinburgh than it was across the

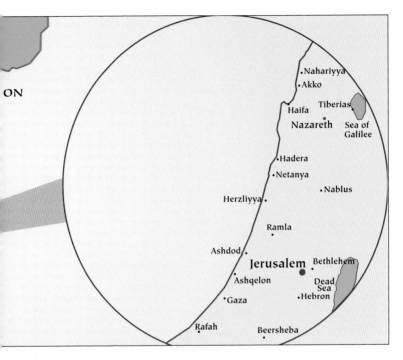

whole of Palestine.) But the extraordinary thing was that Palestine was quite literally on the road to everywhere.

Jesus was brought up in Nazareth - a little village in a dip of the hills. But if Jesus climbed the hill behind Nazareth he would see the road that led from Egypt, right up along the coast, past the Sea of Galilee, away to Damascus and Syria and the Far East. That road was called the Road of the Sea. It was a road by which the caravans and the merchantmen travelled, and if Jesus were to climb the hilltop at Nazareth, he would see the caravans and the merchantmen coming up from Egypt. That is the road by which Joseph's brothers sold him to go down as a slave into Egypt.

If Jesus were to go up that hilltop and if this time instead of turning south he were to turn north, he would see in the distance Ptolemais, the seaport, which the Crusaders knew as Acre. He would see the road which went direct to the east, out to Parthia and the final bounds of the

Roman Empire. On that road once again he would see the caravans and the merchantmen, and the Roman legions clanking out to the frontier to keep the Roman peace, right out to the ends of the earth.

If instead of turning south and north, Jesus were to turn west, he would see the Mediterranean and the ships sailing to Italy, to Greece, to Spain and even to Britain (for by this time the Phoenicians were getting their tin from the mines in Cornwall and sailing it back).

Jesus was there at Nazareth and the ends of the earth came, as it were, to his own back door. He had only to climb that hilltop in Nazareth and all these roads were converging on him. The thoughts of a boy are long, long thoughts, and who shall say that even then Jesus was not thinking 'a world for God'?

A Working Man's Home

Above all, Jesus had the preparation of his own home, One of the things that strikes anyone as being very surprising is why, if Jesus was to be the Saviour of the world, he spent thirty of these thirty-three years in Nazareth. Almost certainly what happened was that Joseph died when Jesus was still quite young, and Jesus had to take over the support of his mother and of his younger brothers and sisters, and of the home. Jesus once told a parable about a servant who was being praised. The master says to the servant: 'You've done well in a few things, I'm going to give a lot of things into your charge.' That was autobiography, for Jesus could never have become the Saviour of the world unless he had been the wage-earner of Nazareth. He had to do the little job well, before the big job could be given to him.

We slander Jesus a little when we call him a carpenter. He was what the Greeks call a *tekton*, and *tekton*, in Greek, meant early on - in Homer, for instance - a shipbuilder. And the *tekton* was much more than a carpenter. In many a Scottish village in the old days, and still to this day, there was a man with the minimum of tools, perhaps just a couple of chisels, and a hammer and a saw, and a set-square, and with this he would build you a house, or build you a bridge, or build you a coffin, or build you a table, or build you a chair. He would do anything - a craftsman in whose hands metal and wood became plastic and obedient. That is what Jesus was.

There is a legend which tells us that he made the best ox-yokes in the whole of Galilee, and that people beat a track to the door of Jesus of Nazareth to buy the ox-yokes that he made. In those days they had trade signs and beside the trade signs they had claims, as it were, for what they were going to do. It has been suggested that over Jesus' carpenter's shop there was a yoke, and above it there was the sentence: 'My yokes fit well'. Jesus was later to say: 'Come unto me all ye that labour or are heavy laden, and take my yoke upon you, for my yoke is easy.' Now that does not mean that it is light and no bother. It is 'easy' in the sense that a pair of shoes are easy or a coat is easy, well-fitting: 'My yokes fit well'.

This of course means that Jesus was a working man. He knew the awkward narky customer, he knew the man who wouldn't pay his bills, he knew the kind of day when the devil got into the wood and the chisel and the saw, and when nothing would go right. He had done a day's work. Just a very short time ago I had half a dozen or so students in my house one evening, and we were discussing the training for the ministry. They were talking about how inadequate, in an industrial situation, the present training for the ministry is. Most of them had worked in industry. They were saying we ought to know more about industry and so forth and so on, and one of them turned to me all of a sudden and said, 'Dr Barclay, have you ever done an honest day's work in your life?' Well, I know what he meant, but if he had said that to Jesus, Jesus could have said, 'Yes - that's my job.'

Jesus also knew what it was to be a member of a big family. He had plenty of brothers and sisters; he knew the stresses and the strains which come of living together. Jesus called God 'Father', but in Gethsemane he said *Abba*, and we are told in Romans 8 and Galatians 4 that we can call God *Abba*. Now *Abba* is the word by which a little Jewish boy calls his father in the home circle. If you go to Jerusalem today, or any Jewish home, you hear the shout *Abba*, *Abba* ringing through the house, the little boy calling on his father. And if you came across it anywhere else, you would translate it 'Daddy'. That is the name Jesus gave to God. What a compliment to Joseph! This is where Jesus got his idea of fatherhood. What a wonderful father Joseph must have been!

There were two other things there in the home at Nazareth that Jesus would see. Every Jew had to wear what were called in the Old Testament 'fringes'. The fringe was a tassel at each end of his robe, and the tassel was made of white threads with one blue thread intertwined through them. The idea was that every time a Jew put on his clothes in the morning he would see the fringe and he would say to himself, 'I'm God's man'. And every time he took them off at night, he would see the fringe and he would say 'I'm God's man'. Night and morning he would see this.

Then in every Jewish house (and you will see it to this day) on the doorpost there was what was called the *Mezuzah* - a little cylindrical box with a little hole in the centre. Inside the box there are certain passages of Scripture, and the Scripture is so written that at the little hole the name of God is seen on the paper. The devout Jew, every time he goes out and in, will touch it with his finger and then touch his lips, remembering God.

A Crisis in the Temple

So Jesus grew up, and he came to the age of twelve. Now when a Jewish boy reaches twelve, he becomes a man and he takes certain tasks upon himself. In the time of Jesus one of the tasks was to attend the great festivals, Pentecost, Tabernacles and the Passover. So Jesus came to the age when he had to attend the Passover, and he would learn all about it. For six weeks before, this was the lesson in school and the sermon in the Synagogue. Jesus saw the workmen working on the roads to make them smooth for the people to walk to the Feast. His whole heart was thrilled. He was going to the Holy City; he was going to the Passover - the greatest of all Feasts. The pilgrims marched up there, singing 'I joyed when to the House of God, go up they said to me'.

The main thing about the Passover was the lamb. You did not buy your lamb in a butcher's shop. The lamb was a sacrifice. You took the lamb to the Temple and had it killed there and then you got it back. But the blood belonged to God and had to be offered to God, and so you led the animal to the barrier. Between you and the altar was a double line of priests. Some of them took the lamb and slit its throat. They poured the

Mezuzah on doorpost

blood into a golden bowl. The bowl was passed up the chain of priests; the blood was thrown on to the altar; then the bowl came back.

In the year 64 there was a Governor of Palestine called Cestius. Cestius wanted to convince Nero how important Palestine was and how important the Passover Feast was. To do this he took a census of the lambs killed at the Passover Feast in AD64. He wanted really to prove how many people were there. There had to be ten people for every lamb, and so for the number of pilgrims you have to multiply by ten. In that one year the number of lambs killed was 256,500.

Imagine what the Temple Court was like - reeking, ankle-deep in blood, with this crimson tide of the blood of the lambs flowing! And surely the young Jesus says, 'People are looking for God, that's what they came here for, not this bloody sacrifice.' Jesus says, 'There's no God there.' It was the biggest disillu sion that had ever hit a boy in history. *No God there.*

There was another thing happened at the Passover time. Only during Passover week the Sanhedrin met in public and discussed in public. So Jesus went there. He thought the priests in the Temple had failed him - no God there. And he thought: 'I'll maybe get God here, in the discussions of the theologians.' And he went and found it uninteresting, irrelevant. They were discussing how far you could walk on the Sabbath; what weight of a burden you could carry on the Sabbath; this ruling, that exception; next letter and comma, and so forth and so on - useless. And Jesus listened, and again he was utterly disillusioned. People are looking for God - this is what they're getting! *No God there, no God there.*

So he had gone first of all to the Temple and the sacrifice - no God in that crimson tide. He had gone to the theologians and listened - no God in these arid arguments. And suddenly the thought just hit him clean between the eyes: *you've got to bring them to God, you!* Now he knew his task. He knew neither the why, nor the when, nor the how. But destiny had spoken to him, he knew he had to bring men to God. So he waited, in the Temple.

His parents went away without him. I don't blame his parents at all for not missing him. When the caravans got started the women and the children started much earlier than the men because they could not walk as fast, and the men started perhaps hours later, and they did not all meet up again till the first encampment in the evening time. And so Joseph thought Jesus was with Mary, and Mary thought he was with Joseph, and neither missed him until the first evening encampment. So they came rushing back to Jerusalem and they searched.

Finally, after all the search, they came upon the boy in the Temple, and Mary came up to him and said, 'Why have you done this? Your father and I have been desperately worried and we've searched for you everywhere.'

Jesus said, 'Didn't you know that I was bound to be in my Father's House?'

Do you see how gently, but absolutely definitely, he takes the name 'father' from Joseph and gives it to God? Jesus knows, not everything, far from it, but he knows that in one way or another he is in this perfectly definite relationship to God - a relationship which is unique; a relationship which is his relationship.

There is a long way to go yet, and a lot to learn yet. He goes back to school; he goes back to work in the carpenter's shop; he goes back to being obedient to his parents in the day's work; he goes back to the hidden life and the ordinary things. He serves and works and is obedient a long time ... a long time - eighteen years, *another eighteen years*. And then when Jesus is thirty, suddenly the hour strikes.

The Hour Strikes
The hour strikes with the emergence of a man called John the Baptist. Down there by the Jordan, John was baptizing them in thousands. What was odd about this was that never in history had a Jew been baptized before. Baptism was to wash away and to cleanse pollution and stain and sin. But were not the Jews God's chosen people? They did not need to be baptized! Gentiles, yes - but not Jews. But now for the first time in history Jews were submitting to being baptized.

Suddenly Jesus sees it. He hears the call. The hour has struck; here is a sense of sin; here is a summons to God. Jesus goes to the river; a voice comes to him. The voice says, 'This is my beloved Son in whom I am well pleased.'

The River Jordan

Now that is two texts put together. 'This is my beloved Son' is Psalm 2, verse 7, and it was used at the coronation of every king. It meant might, majesty, power, royalty. 'In whom I am well pleased' is Isaiah 42, verse 1 - part of the picture which culminates in Isaiah 53, of the servant who was wounded for our transgressions and bruised for our iniquities and on whom the chastisement of our peace fell.

Two things: royalty, and at the same time blood and sweat and tears. Jesus saw it. He saw kingship in front of him, but kingship at a cost. And so he was out upon his task.

2

CONFLICT

If a man is going to start out on a great work, it is an absolute first essential that he should know just what he is trying to do, and just how he is going to do it. This is precisely the problem which faced Jesus. The hour had struck in the coming of John the Baptist, he knew that it was time to go out to bring God to men and to bring men to God. But the first thing he had to decide was just how he was going to do this, and this brought to him his first conflict, because the temptation story is the story of Jesus deciding just how he was going to set about the task which God had given him to do.

A Picture of Jesus Tested

There are certain things about this temptation story which it would be well to notice before we look at the story in detail.

This story might be called the most sacred story in the New Testament – for this reason, that there is only one possible origin and source for this story, and that is Jesus himself. No one was there; he was alone in the wilderness. Therefore this story must have been told by Jesus himself to his disciples on some occasion when he wished to help them.

But in a sense the word 'temptation' is very misleading because the Greek word that is used does not quite mean temptation, and temptation does not mean what we think it means in the Bible's Authorized Version in the seventeenth century. We take this word 'temptation' to mean, entirely, seduction to sin. That is not altogether what it means in the Bible, and it is certainly not altogether what it means in this passage. If you look up the Authorized Version, Genesis 22, verse 1, that verse starts: 'And God did tempt Abraham'. This is the

THE NAMES AND TITLES OF JESUS

Jesus

The Greek version of three common Hebrew names, Joshua, Jehoshua and Jeshua. It means "The Lord (Yahweh) is my help" or "Yahweh rescues."

Lord

Signifying Christ's rule over all. Used very frequently by Paul.

Son of man

Used by Jesus of himself to include both meanings as found in the Old Testament - both very human (as in Ezekiel) and also divine.

I am

The personal name of God as revealed to Moses at the burning bush. In Hebrew, Yahweh. Used by Jesus of himself this name provoked the charge of blasphemy.

Messiah

Hebrew title meaning 'anointed', its Greek equivalent is 'Christ'. Open to misinterpretation during his lifetime, Jesus largely kept his messiahship secret.

Son of God

While all Christians, as God's children, are sons of God, Jesus is The Son of God. He addressed God as 'Father' and has a unique relationship with Him.

Son of David

Arising out of the promise to David that his throne would be established for ever, the Jewish people looked for a 'son of David' who would be their Messiah. Born in Bethlehem, David's city, Jesus was seen as the Son of David by the first Christians.

The lamb

Coming from the lamb used in sacrifices, especially at Passover, this title signifies the spilling of blood in order to save God's people from death.

the bread of life.   John 6:35
                                          (also John 6:48, 51)

the light of the world.   John 8:12
                                          (also John 9:5; 12:35; see also John 1:4)

the door for the sheep.   John 10:7
                                          (also John 10:9)

the good shepherd.   John 10:11
                                          (see also Hebrews 13:20; 1 Peter 5:4)

the resurrection and the life.   John 11:25
                                          (see also John 1:4; 5:26; 14:6)

the way and the truth and the life.   John 14:6
                                          (see also John 10:9; 8:32; 1:4; 11:25)

the true vine.   John 15:1

prelude to the story of Abraham and the sacrifice of Isaac. Of course you cannot possibly think that this means that God was trying to seduce Abraham into sin. What it does mean is: 'And God did test Abraham'. Temptation is, far more, testing. It is the sending of a man through an ordeal to see whether he is a fit instrument for the task that has been given to him to do. And so we might rather call this story the testing of Jesus, to see if he would choose the right method for the work that lies ahead of him.

We are not to think of this story, as it were, happening externally – Satan coming up in a suit, or in a physical form, or anything like that. We are to think of this story all going on inside Jesus' head. You see that straight away when you come to the end. You hear about Jesus being taken up into a high mountain from which he could see all the kingdoms of the world. Now of course there is no mountain high enough in all the world to see the whole world. This was going on inside Jesus' mind. That is the way temptation works. When you are tempted, pictures rise in your mind – pictures of things you would like to do, pictures of things you should not do. That is what happened to Jesus. And we are not to think of the temptation story as one temptation, finish, curtain: second temptation, finish, curtain: third temptation ... We are to think of Jesus, over a long period, going through this battle with the thoughts and ideas in his mind that would not be stilled.

Did you ever notice when this temptation story happened? It happened immediately after the baptism of Jesus. The baptism of Jesus had been his great moment when there came the voice of God: 'You are my beloved Son, in you I am well pleased.' And then, as Mark has it, 'immediately the Spirit tossed him out into the wilderness'. *Immediately!* You see what this means. Immediately after the great moment there came the conflict with temptation.

There is a certain kind of evangelist who says to you: 'Accept Jesus Christ and you will have rest and peace and joy.' Now of course there is a certain amount of truth in that, but it's a half-truth, and like all half-truths, it is dangerous – because it is also true that when you accept Jesus Christ your troubles start. Up until that time you have been satisfied with much lower standards, conduct and values. But now you are faced with life as a much bigger battle. And so you see that after the big moment, temptation is likely to come. After the big moment the conflict came to Jesus. What happened to Jesus will very likely happen to us, and if it does happen to us we are not to think that there is anything wrong with it at all.

There is a very difficult situation indeed for Jesus here. He did not, as it were, start from scratch with his thinking. His aim was to bring God to men and to bring men to God, but he was not the only person to think about this and he was not the only person who had set out to do this. The Jews were actually expecting someone who would do it – they called this someone the Messiah. They had their ideas of what the Messiah should be like – a person of might and majesty and power who would raise up the armies of Israel; who would lead them through Palestine, throwing the Romans out of the country, and who would lead the Jews to world power and world dominion. Jesus, having been brought up on this – on the idea of a Messiah who would be a conquering, majestic, mighty, powerful king – has to decide: 'Am I going to be like that?' 'Am I going to be a great commander leading armies to victory?' 'Am I going to accept this popular idea or is there some other way?' At his temptation we see Jesus deciding which of these ways he will take.

In order to settle this Jesus wanted to be alone, and he went away into the desert. This desert was between Jerusalem and the Dead Sea, and it is one of the most terrible deserts in the world – so much so that people called it by the name *Jeshimon*, which means 'the devastation'. We usually think of a wilderness as being sandy, but this was not a desert of sand, it was a limestone desert, covered and carpeted with little blocks of limestone. Across it ran the ridges and the hills all contorted and twisted, with parts of them broken and jagged like a decayed tooth. When you walked across it or when you rode a horse across it, the noise of your feet or of the horse's hooves sounded hollow. It was like walking across an oven that glistened and shimmered in the heat, and there was never anybody there.

Three Wrong Ideas

So Jesus went there to be alone, to fight this conflict out and to decide just what he was going to do. But before the main temptations came to him, there came a temptation that was in some ways the most serious of all, because twice the tempting voice said to him, 'If you are the Son of God, turn these stones into bread ... If you are the Son of God, do this ... '

If! This voice was saying to Jesus, 'Are you quite sure that you are the Son of God? Don't you think you might be kidding yourself on? Don't you think you might be mistaken? Don't you think this might be one great big delusion? Are you quite sure?' This was an attempt to throw doubt on Jesus' call. If Jesus had accepted doubt in his call, then he was finished, for doubting his call would paralyse all action. And so he was faced first of all with the problem of certainty, the problem of being sure, quite sure, that he was doing what God wanted him to do.

So the temptations come to Jesus – really ideas rising in his mind of how he might do his work. The first idea is this – he looks at the ground and it is carpeted with little round blocks of stone exactly like little loaves. The Palestinian loaf is not at all like the loaf that we use in this country – the Palestinian loaf is like a little breakfast roll, or even a Vienna roll. The boy whose picnic lunch Jesus used to feed the five thousand had five loaves and two small fishes. But not even a boy will eat five loaves for lunch when they are our size! They were five little rolls. Those little limestone stones were exactly like loaves and rolls ... and the tempting voice said, 'Turn these into bread.' Jesus says, 'I want men to follow me'; and the idea comes to him – 'Give them material things, give them more food, give them better houses, give them more money, give them better jobs, give them a society in which they can say, "We've never had it so good" and then they will follow you to the end of time.' Jesus says, 'No, give people all the material things in the world and you don't fully satisfy them – the only thing that will really satisfy them is the word of God, and that's what I bring.'

Then there comes to Jesus this second idea, which is – 'Give them sensations, give them wonders, give them signs, baffle them, paralyse them with wonder.' Two pictures come into Jesus' mind.

The first was the east side of the Temple. The east side of the Temple came straight up – the hill came up like a precipice, and then in line with the precipice there rose the wing of the Temple, and on top of that the tower, and from the top of the tower down to the Kedron valley below was a drop of 430 feet, and it was said no one could look down that without being dizzy. Jesus had the idea, 'What about floating down and landing at the bottom unhurt? That would shake them, that would make them follow me!'

The Temple, looking down over the Kedron valley, 430 feet below

Again, Jesus saw in his mind's eye the Tower of Antonia in the Temple. It overlooked the Temple court, and twice a day the court was jammed tight with people at the morning and evening sacrifice. The idea comes to Jesus, 'What about jumping down just when the sacrifice is going on, floating down and arriving unharmed? *That* would be a sensation!' And then Jesus says, 'No – you don't want to follow a policy of sensations, because you know yourself that a nine-days' wonder *is* a nine-days' wonder, and on the tenth day no one will cross the street to see it. If you commit yourself to a policy of sensations you have to offer bigger and better sensations all the time – there is no future in that.' Jesus says, 'That is not the way to look at God. That is trying to see how far you can go with God, trying to see how far you can get away with it.' He says, 'That is not faith, but folly. That is not the way to do it.'

Then there comes the third idea. Jesus sees the world stretched out before him – and nobody knew better than Jesus how worldly the world was – and the idea comes to him, 'Now why shouldn't I compromise just a little, why shouldn't I drop my demands just a little, why shouldn't I meet the world halfway, why shouldn't I say there's good in all religions? Let's make a kind of amalgam of the whole lot.' As was written on a temple in one of the Roman cities, 'God is a name which all religions share'; another temple had 'Surely there cannot be one way to so great a goal?' And Jesus says, 'No, God is God, the devil is the devil; right is right, wrong is wrong; there is only one way, and I take that.'

Jesus and the Law

Now Jesus is committed – once and for all he is committed against the way of might and majesty and armies and political power. Blood and sweat and tears – he is committed to the way of suffering. But the temptations lead to more conflict almost immediately. If Jesus was going to take this way, he was bound to be in trouble, and to be in trouble straight away.

The most precious thing the Jews had was *the law*. The Jew said, 'Oh how I love thy law!' And he did. The Jew uses the word 'law' in two senses. First he uses it to mean the written law in the Old Testament, namely the Ten Commandments and the first five books of the Bible.

Now the law in the Old Testament does not have a multitude of rules and regulations: what it has is great wide principles, and it lays on the individual man, on each and all, the responsibility of fitting these principles to every individual case that comes up. But the Jewish theologians and leaders thought this far too risky. They wanted rules and regulations to meet the needs of every man in every situation – to be able to say this, this, this, in each particular situation. And so, out of the principles they began to extract literally thousands and thousands of rules and regulations; after all, the law was the word of God, therefore complete and perfect, and therefore everything is in it – if not *ex*plicitly, then *im*plicitly, and one has to dig it out.

Take the Jewish law of the Sabbath and just see how this worked. The Sabbath law in the Old Testament says quite simply, 'Remember the Sabbath day to keep it holy,' and then it says you must not do any work on the Sabbath day, neither you nor your servants nor your animals nor anyone. It was just to be a great day of rest. Here is the great wide principle. And then the Jewish lawyers got to work on this and they asked, 'This Sabbath, *when* does it begin?' (They had no clocks or watches as today.) 'We must have some definition ... The Sabbath begins when three stars come out.'

As for 'Thou shalt do no work on the Sabbath' – the lawyers asked, 'What is work?' and they then laid down thirty-nine different 'fathers of work' – classifications of work: reaping, spinning, winnowing, hoeing, threshing, beating the corn, carrying a burden, lighting a fire – all kinds of things. Then they took these and subdivided them, with a great passion for definition. Some of the things which follow will seem fantastic and ludicrous, but we should remember two things – first, this to the Jew was serving God, doing what God wanted; secondly, in doing this the Jew had to exercise a self-discipline and a self-control that most Christians do not exercise at all. It was good then, even if misguided.

Let us see what they did. One of the things that was forbidden was tying a knot – to tie a knot on the Sabbath day was to work. Now we know the question which follows: 'What is a knot?' The answer was – anything you can tie with two hands. If you can tie it with one hand, all is well – it is not a sin. Then of course, in the old days, there were no such things as zip fasteners, and a woman simply could not dress herself on the Sabbath without tying knots. She was therefore allowed to tie a knot in her shift or in her girdle, or in the cap she wore on her hair, or anything like that. Now what happens? It is the Sabbath – they forgot to draw water and they have to lower a bucket down into the well. They cannot tie a knot in the rope – it is the Sabbath. But they can take a woman's girdle and tie a knot in it and let the bucket down in the well – that is absolutely all right!

Again, take the case of carrying a burden. We all know the question without my telling: 'What is a burden?' And we get a long list – pages and pages of it: anything the weight of a dried fig; enough paper to write 'Hear, O Israel'; enough wine for one swallow; enough oil to anoint a small member (what is a small member? – it is the little toe of a baby three days old!); and on and on and on. And so they argued. Can a man go out with a wooden leg on the Sabbath, or is he carrying a burden? Can a woman go out with false hair on the Sabbath or is she carrying a burden? Or can a man pick up a child on the Sabbath or is he carrying a burden? No, he can pick up the child all right, but not if the child has a stone in his hand – it's a burden then. But – what is a stone? Anything big enough to throw at a bird. On and on it goes.

Then again, one has to move some furniture on the Sabbath. Well , one can move a chair so long as it has *two* cross-pieces – if it has three cross-pieces, it becomes a ladder and cannot be moved. And one must *lift* it – one cannot drag it because if one drags it it leaves two furrows in the earthen floor – and that is technically ploughing!

Now we laugh at this, yes, we laugh. But remember, this was life and death – remember that. If we were as careful about our religion, we would be a lot more religious.

Jesus and Jewish Religion
Again, there was the question of healing. Of course it was forbidden to heal on the Sabbath – that was to work. You could take such steps as would stop a man getting any worse, and of course if he was in danger of his life, you could do something. You could put a plain bandage on to his hand, but not a bandage with ointment. You could put ordinary cotton wool into his ear, but not medicated cotton wool. A man with

JESUS AND THE JEWISH LAW

The fulfilment of the law:
"You have heard that it was said…" Matthew 5:17-48

Surpassing the law:

touching the 'unclean'	Matthew 8:1-3; Mark 1:40
eating with 'sinner'	Matthew 9:10-13; Luke 5:29-32; Luke 15:1-2
not fasting	Matthew 9:14-17; Mark 2:18; Luke 5:33-35
'working' on the Sabbath	Matthew 12:9-14; Mark 3:1-2; Luke 6:6-11; 13:10-14; 14:1-4; John 5:8-10; 9:13-14
not washing before eating	Luke 11:37-38
associating with a Samaritan	John 4:7-9

toothache could take a drink of vinegar, but he could not draw it through his teeth because that would be curing the toothache, and that would be to work.

Or take the case of writing. It was a sin to write on the Sabbath two letters of the alphabet; not two letters but two letters of the alphabet. But – it was only a sin if you wrote them in something permanent, and if you wrote them with a pen in the normal way. If you wrote them in fruit juice or if you wrote them in the sand or in the dust, that was all right, not permanent; if you wrote them with your elbow or if you wrote them with your nose, that was all right, not the normal way of writing. And the two letters must be able to be read at the same time. If you could not read them at the same time it was all right – one instance cited is if you wrote one on the roof of a house and one on the pavement!

Now this, for the Jew, was religion – his whole life was governed by this. Do we see what that means? It means that if all this is right, Jesus is quite desperately wrong. This is the clash of two kinds of religion. It is the clash between 'Thou shalt, thou shalt not' religion and between religion which says, 'Love God and love your fellow men.' Now, if Jesus was right, all this was completely and totally irrelevant. Obviously the people who had loved this kind of thing thought Jesus was a bad and a dangerous man, and thought that the sooner this man was out of the way, the better.

Then there were the priests, 6,000 of them. Obviously 6,000 priests cannot all serve at the one time, so they were divided into twenty-four different courses, and they served only twice a year in the Temple. The only time the whole 6,000 were on duty was at the Feast of Tabernacles, the Feast of Pentecost and the Passover. The priests worked five weeks in the year, that was all. And the sacrifices were not all burned on the altar, not anything like all of them – the priests had some of them and the worshippers had some. The priests were the pampered religious aristocracy, working five weeks in the year and living on the fat of the land. When Jesus comes and says 'I will have mercy and not sacrifice', the priests say, 'For goodness sake let's get rid of this man or we've lost our job and our comfort.' They must do something.

Now to say all this is not anti-semitic. We would have done exactly the same, and we would do precisely and exactly the same if Jesus came back. In the last century a very muslin-and-lace refined lady came to Carlyle and said to him, 'Mr Carlyle, don't you think the Jews were terrible crucifying Jesus? Don't you think if he came back we would give him such a welcome?' Carlyle said, 'Madam, if he came back preaching doctrines palatable to the higher orders, I think I should receive from you a card to a reception to meet our Saviour. But if he came back preaching his sublime doctrines you would say, "Take him to Newgate and hang him."' (And so we would.) This is not anti-semitic, blaming the Jews, it is simply saying that the Jews were the representatives of humanity.

The Grotto of the Agony, Gethsemane

The Last Conflict

There was one last conflict, and in many ways this was the most terrible of all. It was the conflict at Gethsemane. There Jesus could quite certainly have turned back. If he could not have turned back, then the whole scene is no more than play-acting. He nearly turned back. He did not want to die – no one wants to die at thirty-three. He did not want to die on a cross – the most humiliating and agonizing of deaths which men have ever devised for a fellow man. He prayed to God to take this away.

I can only guess what happened to Jesus, and this is what I think happened. (Some may not agree, but for me this is very precious.) I think Jesus knew he had to go on, I think he knew this was the will of God, but I think he did not know *why*. He knew he had to suffer, he just did not know why. He was going to do it all right, even if he did not understand. Now one of the hardest things in life is to accept what we cannot understand. Jesus did that at Gethsemane. Thank God he did it – we all have to do it, but it's easier when we see our Lord doing it fist.

So Jesus had the three conflicts. He had the conflict over the right way (the Jews thought they knew it), the conflict with orthodoxy (they thought he was a bad man), and the conflict with himself. He won them all and went on.

3

RECOGNITION

It is always a supremely interesting thing to try to follow the life of a great man from day to day and if possible from hour to hour and from event to event, but a still more fascinating and interesting thing is to follow not the events of a man's life but to try to follow his thoughts - to try to get inside his mind, to see how it works, and to see the things which were really the dynamic driving powers in his life and in his work. That is what we shall try to do with Jesus.

The Kingdom of God

Now we can do that along two lines, one line being the line of something that he himself said and the other line something that was said about him by somebody who knew him probably better than any other person in the New Testament.

We begin with what Jesus himself said. When he emerged in the public view he said, 'The Kingdom of Heaven is at hand.' He came to proclaim and to announce that the *Kingdom of Heaven*, or the *Kingdom of God*, had come.

In English this is just slightly misleading, because for us the word 'kingdom' often has a geographical reference. We usually think of a kingdom as an area of land - the Kingdom of England or the Kingdom of Scotland or the Kingdom of Belgium. We talk of the length and breadth of the kingdom. But when this word kingdom is used on the lips of Jesus, the 'Kingdom of God', he is not referring to anything in the geographical sense. He means rather the *kingship* of God, and if we were to put this in a way which would avoid all possible troubles and mistakes, we would put it thus: 'God is about to begin his reign' or 'God is about to begin his rule'.

This is the essential message of Jesus - *God is about to begin his rule!* Here is our starting-point to find a definition for this phrase 'the Kingdom of God' and for the meaning of it. We could start with this perfectly general rule, that if one is going to be a member of any kingdom, a citizen of any state, one must begin by agreeing to be obedient to the rules and the laws and the constitution of that kingdom. Therefore the membership of any kingdom involves obedience; obedience and citizenship of any kingdom go hand in hand.

Now we must try to get a better definition of the kingdom than that, a closer definition. All Hebrew and Jewish writing has one tendency - to what is technically known as parallelism. This means that the Jews nearly always said everything twice; they say something and then you get a break, and then they repeat the thing and the second version amplifies or expands or even defines the first. So, for instance, in the Psalm 46 we have:

> The Lord of hosts is with us;
> The God of Jacob is our refuge.

Or in Psalm 23:

> He maketh me to lie down in green pastures;
> He leadeth me beside the still waters.

One thing, then a break - then the second and parallel thing, amplifying or defining or expanding the first thing.

So there are two phrases in the Lord's Prayer, two petitions side by side:

> Thy kingdom come;
> Thy will be done in earth as it is in Heaven.

We assume that here we have a case of this Hebrew parallelism and that the second thing defines or expands or develops or explains the first thing:

> Thy kingdom come,
> Thy will be done in earth as it is in Heaven.

THE KINGDOM OF GOD
THE KINGDOM OF HEAVEN
SAYINGS OF JESUS

...the kingdom of heaven is near (Matthew 4:17; 10:7)

...theirs is the kingdom of God (Matthew 5:3,10; Luke 6:20)

...seek first the kingdom of God (Matthew 6:33; Luke 12:31)

Not everyone ... will enter the kingdom of heaven (Matthew 7:21)

...the feast...in the kingdom of heaven (Matthew 8:11; Luke 13:29; 14:15)

...the kingdom of God has come upon you (Matthew 12:28; Luke 11:20)

The secrets of the kingdom of heaven have been given to you

        (Matthew 13:11-23; Mark 4:1-20; Luke 8:1-15)

The kingdom of heaven is like.....

    a man who sowed good seed (Matthew 13:18; Mark 4:26)

    a mustard seed (Matthew 13:31; Mark 4:30)

    yeast (Matthew 13:33)

    treasure (Matthew 13:44)

    a fine pearl (Matthew 13:45)

    a net (Matthew 13:47)

From this second line expanding and explaining the first we get this definition: *The kingdom of God is a society upon earth where God's will is as perfectly done as it is in Heaven.* This is the all-important definition with which we start.

Now immediately we lay that down, certain things become clear and certain things become challenges as well. There is one rather mysterious thing about the kingdom in the New Testament, at least at first sight:

...the keys of the kingdom of heaven (Matthew 16:19)

...the greatest in the kingdom of heaven (Matthew 18:1-4)

...to enter the kingdom of God (Matthew 19:14; Mark 10:23-25; Luke 18:24-25)

...are entering the kingdom of God ahead of you (Matthew 21:31)

The kingdom of God will be taken away from you (Matthew 21:43)

The kingdom of God is near (Mark 1:15; Luke 10:9,11; 21:31)

...see the kingdom of God come with power (Mark 9:1)

...better to enter the kingdom of God (Mark 9:47-48)

...the kingdom of God belongs to such as these (Mark 10:13-15; Luke 18:16-17)

You are not far from the kingdom of God (Mark 12:34)

...the good news of the kingdom of God (Luke 4:43; 16:16)

...before they see the kingdom of God (Luke 9:27)

...go and proclaim the kingdom of God (Luke 9:60-62)

...the kingdom of God is within you (Luke 17:20-21)

...for the sake of the kingdom of God (Luke 18:29-30)

...no one can see the kingdom of God unless he is born again (John 3:3-5)

and that is how the New Testament manages to speak of the kingdom as past, present and future all at the one time. For instance, we read in the New Testament of Abraham and Isaac and Jacob and all the patriarchs as being of the kingdom, and as they lived a very long time ago the kingdom has therefore been lasting for thousands and thousands of years. Then Jesus says that 'the kingdom is *within* you' or 'the kingdom is *among* you' - so the kingdom is here and now. And yet

Jesus goes on to say that we are to pray, 'Thy Kingdom come' - so the kingdom is in the future. How can the kingdom be at one and the same time, past, present and future? Well, when we grasp this idea that the kingdom and the will of God are identical, we can say this: that *any* man who has done the will of God at *any* time is in the kingdom. He who has done the will of God, he who does it, and he who will do it - every one of them is in the kingdom. Citizenship and obedience are synonymous, and whenever you do the will of God you are *in* the kingdom of God, then and there.

But further, a certain challenge appears in this. The minute we see that this idea of the kingdom is all tied up with the doing of the will of God, then we begin to see that the kingdom is not a thing of nations and races and empires and politics - the kingdom is an intensely personal thing which has to do with each and all of us. Rather than being keen to talk of bringing in the kingdom by this, that and the next political means or party, we shall see it as much nearer home than that. If doing the will of God and being in the kingdom are synonymous, we might adapt the Chinese Christian's prayer: 'O Lord, revive thy Church, beginning with me.' We might well pray: 'O Lord, bring in thy Kingdom, beginning with me.' Help me to make this commitment which is necessary for the coming of the kingdom!

Doing God's Will

When we see this idea of the will of God and the kingdom being one and the same, there are certain difficult sayings of Jesus which become understandable. For instance, there is that saying of Jesus which sounds so very fierce and savage: 'If your hand is in your way causing you to stumble, cut it off and throw it away ... If your eye is making you sin, tear it out and throw it away, for it is better to enter the kingdom with one hand or with one eye than to be cast with your whole body intact into hellfire.' When Jesus said that, he meant - if you want to put it into simpler and less alarming language - simply this: It is worth any sacrifice to do the will of God; it is worth any surgical excision from life, of your desires and your ambitions and your plans and your aims, to do the will of God.

Jesus tells a story, one of his best-known stories, about the man who spent his whole life searching for pearls. This merchantman travelled all over the country, perhaps even the length of Britain here, searching for pearls and then, presumably near the end of his life, he came upon *the* perfect pearl, the most beautiful pearl in the world - what does he do? He takes and he sells every single thing that he has and he buys this pearl of great price. Jesus says, 'The kingdom is like that.' He meant just this, that the kingdom is worth everything.

Put it the other way - to do the will of God is worth everything in life, is a bigger thing than everything else put together. When we say that, of course we do not mean that if we do the will of God there will be no more trouble, no bother, no unpopularity, no difficulty, no obstacles. It does not mean that we will have material prosperity and happiness in that sense of the term. What it does mean, to put it very simply, is that we will have satisfaction which we will never get any other way, and we know that. We know perfectly well that if we do the right thing, even if that right thing has cost us something, we have a deep abiding satisfaction. And we know quite well that if we know what the right thing is and we fail to do it - even if saving ourselves an awful lot of bother and giving us far more ease and comfort - we have a vague, gnawing dissatisfaction at the bottom of our heart and in our life. Obviously, doing the will of God, doing the right thing, is the thing which gives satisfaction and peace.

We begin then with this, that 'to be a member of the kingdom' and 'to do the will of God' are one and the same. Obedience and citizenship of the kingdom are the same! You may say, 'I agree that it's all-important to do the will of God - I can see this quite clearly. This is the most important thing, the most precious thing. I can see how this would bring me happiness and satisfaction and peace of mind. But, *how can I know this will of God?* Where do I get it?' For man, being man, can never reach up into God. If the knowledge of God has ever come to man that knowledge must have come down; there is no climbing up to get it. Anything that we discover must be already given - we discover things not by speculation, but as they are revealed. And we ask, How am I to know this will of God, where do I get it? Which brings us to this - *there is only one person who has ever perfectly done the will of God, and that one person is Jesus.*

Jesus said, 'My meat and drink is to do the will of my Father.' Jesus is the embodiment of the will of God - Jesus is therefore the embodiment of the kingdom. If you want to see what the kingdom is like, look at Jesus. The kingdom came in Jesus Christ. Other people do the will of God spasmodically, now and again - we all do it now and again. The world does the will of God in parts, but in Jesus you see the will of God perfectly done - you see that, in Jesus, the kingdom has come.

Now this is precisely where Jesus is different from any other teacher. All the rest of us who have to teach, especially those of us who teach young people, are continually having to say 'Don't do as I do, but do as I say'. We're continually having to say to people, 'I'll *tell* you how to do this, but I can't *show* you how to do this.' Emerson once said of Seneca, 'He says the loveliest things. If only he had the right to say them!' Any preacher must feel the stab in that. Robert Louis Stevenson once said of a teacher, 'I cannot hear what you say for listening to what you are.' Any teacher must feel the stab of that. But Jesus was quite clear of this. Jesus can and does say, not simply 'I tell you', but 'I show you what you ought to do.' He came, not just to talk about the kingdom, but to show men what the kingdom is like.

The Word Became Flesh
Here we come to the other thing that was said about Jesus, by the person who knew him best of all. In some ways I think that what I am now going to quote is quite the most important text in the New Testament. It is the text: 'The Word became flesh'. Now there is a difficulty about this text in translation, for this reason. The Greek used for 'Word' is *logos*, and the trouble about this word *logos* is that it has two translations in English, both equally valid, both equally biting, and there is no one English word which covers both of them. That is why Moffatt in his translation of the New Testament does not try to translate; he simply says, 'The *logos* became flesh and dwelt among us' and leaves it at that. We shall look at this word and try to see the two translations and what this tells us about Jesus and about the will of God and our whole Christian life.

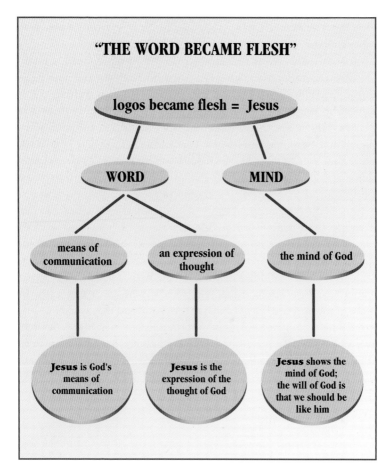

The first translation of *logos* is 'word.' This is the commonest translation. So the text says; Jesus is the word of God come to this world. Now what would you say that a word is? There are two possible definitions.

First of all, a word is *a means of communication*. If I want to communicate with someone, the only way I can do this is through words; words are my medium and my means of communication. If I say then that Jesus is the word of God, I am saying that Jesus is God's means of communication. In Jesus, God speaks; Jesus is God's liaison with men, God's means of communication with men.

But, secondly, a word is more than that. A word is not only a means of communication, often a word is a secondary thing. We have to do something before we speak, or at least we ought to do something before we speak - we ought to think! A word is therefore *an expression of a thought*. I think, and then I speak, and my word is the expression of my thought. If I say that Jesus is the word of God, I say that Jesus is the expression of the thought of God. If you want to see what God is thinking, look at Jesus Christ. If you want to see how the mind of God works, look at Jesus Christ. If you want to get an insight into what you might call the dynamic personality of God, look at Jesus Christ. So that if we say Jesus is the word of God, we are saying that Jesus is God's means of communication, and that Jesus is the expression of the thought of God.

Now we take the other meaning of the word *logos* - 'mind'. Quite commonly, *logos* means mind. The Greeks were fascinated with the order of the universe. They looked at this world and they could not stop marvelling at it - what makes the sun rise and set; what makes the tides ebb and flow; why do spring, summer, autumn and winter come in their unvarying cycle; why is H2O always water? (The Greek would not have known this, but he would have approved of the illustration!) Why is there always the same effect and the same cause and the same reaction from the same action? One of the things that they did use was this. Why, when you plant a turnip seed, do you always get a turnip and not sometimes a carrot? How can you be certain that if you plant the seed you get this thing? How can you be so dependent on the world as that? And the Greeks said, 'This is the mind of God, putting sense into things; this is the mind of God, making an order out of this world.'

There was in Ephesus (the fourth Gospel was written in Ephesus) a very famous teacher called Heraclitus, 600 years before John. He was full of this *logos* - it was part of his life, part of his work, he was always thinking about it. He used to say: 'Everything is in a state of flux.' Nothing stays steady! The illustration he used was, 'You can't step into the same river twice' - step into the river, step out, step in again - it is a different river because the first river has flowed by and left you with another. He said, 'Life is like that, life is a continuous state of flux and yet in spite of that, life is dependable. In spite of that you know where the sun is going to rise tomorrow morning, not only that, you know to the second when it will rise. You know the tides' ebb and flow - you can depend on the seasons. In spite of the flux there's order. What is that order? The mind of God; this is the mind of God interpenetrating the universe.' This is what the Greeks looked for, and John says, 'For 600 years you have been talking about the mind of God - if you want to see the mind of God, *look at Jesus Christ*: here *is* the mind of God.'

How are we to know the will of God? - that was our question. We know the will of God simply by looking at Jesus Christ. And when we see Jesus Christ, we see - what? Someone who fed the hungry, healed the sick, comforted the sad, who was the friend of outcasts and sinners. If this is the mind of God, then the will of God is that we should be exactly the same. We Christians should be like this.

You might think that Christianity necessarily consists in going to church twice on Sunday and in having your freewill offering envelopes in up to date, and attending prayer meetings and Bible Study circles and all the rest of it. The truth is that Christianity does not mean that at all, necessarily. What it *does* mean is loving God and loving men. But you cannot do the one without the other! As John said, if you say you love God and hate your brother, you are a liar, quite wantonly. John says this: the only way you can prove you love God is by loving your fellow man, and this is doing the will of God - just that.

We know there are so many Christians - or so-called Christians - who are not like that at all. They never get drunk; they will never swear; they will not commit adultery; they will pay their debts all right. But if you were in trouble you could never go and put your head on their shoulder and sob out your sorry story. You would freeze to death before you had two sentences spoken! And this is exactly the opposite of what God is like. God is not like that, because Jesus is not like that.

Peter's Recognition

Is there anyone who recognized Jesus for this when he was in this world? For, if Jesus was out to form a kingdom, then obviously what he must

JESUS' JOURNEY TO JERUSALEM

No line is shown on the map because it is not clear from the Gospels exactly which route was taken by Jesus. From the time of his Transfiguration, somewhere in the region of Caesarea Philippi, to his arrest in Jerusalem, he is recorded as being present in a number of places.

1. **Region of Caesarea Philippi**

   Matthew 16:13 - 17:21

   Mark 8:27 - 9:29

   Luke 9:18 - 36

2. **Galilee/Capernaum**

   Matthew 17:22 - 18:35

   Mark 9:30 - 50

3. **Samaria**

   Luke 9:51 - 10:16

4. **Jerusalem**

   Luke 10:25 - 37

5. **Bethany**

   John 11:1 - 46

6. **Peraea**

   Matthew 19:1 - 20:16

   Mark 10:1 - 45

7. **Jericho**

   Matthew 20:29 - 34

   Mark 10:46 - 52

   Luke 18:35 - 19:27

8. **Bethany / Bethphage**

   Matthew 21:1-9

   Mark 11:1-12

   Luke 19:28-44

   John 12:1-11

9. **Jerusalem (further visits to Bethany and the Mount of Olives /Bethphage are recorded in all the Gospels during the last days before Jesus' arrest)**

   Matthew 21:10 ff.

   Mark 11:15 ff.

   Luke 19:45 ff.

   John 12:12 ff.

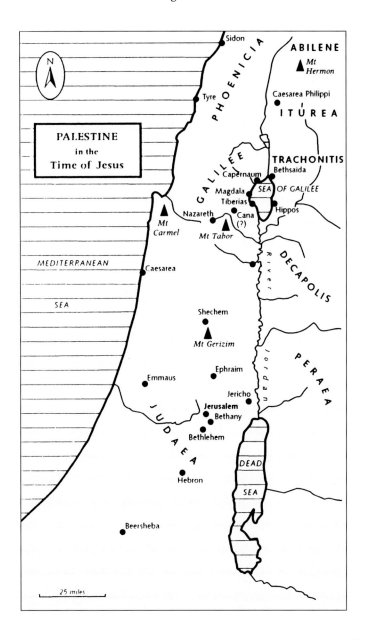

have is *men*. Men are the substance of a kingdom. Whom did he have? Near the end of his life, Jesus was coming to see that he had to know whether he had anyone or not. So he took his disciples away for a time, up to Caesarea Philippi, twenty or thirty miles north of Galilee, and for some days he talked to them.

Just think of this scene. Caesarea Philippi had originally been called Baalinas. It was a place where the worship of Baal centred. Then it was called Paneas, a place where the Greek god Pan had been. It was also known as the source of the Jordan. Finally it was called 'Caesar's city', because Philip had built there a great tremendous white temple to the godhead of Caesar. The gods of Palestine look down, the gods of Greece look down; the history of Israel looks down; the might of imperial Rome and the divinity of Caesar look down. And a penniless Galilean carpenter, an outlaw, going to Jerusalem to die, turns to a group of men in the face of all that and says, 'What are men saying about me?'

They say, 'Some say you're Elijah; some John the Baptist; some Jeremiah; some, one of the prophets.' Now these are all good answers, meant to be compliments, but all human.

Then there was a pause, one of those pauses when history holds its breath, and then Jesus points to the disciples and says, 'You, who do you say that I am?'

Another pause - and back comes the answer from Peter, whose heart was always first in his mouth: 'You are the Christ, the Son of the Living God.' And Jesus knows! Then Jesus says to Peter, 'It was no man who told you this; it was God. And you are Peter, you are the rock (Peter means a rock) - the rock on which I have built my Church.' This means that Peter was the foundation stone of the Christian Church - he was the first person to discover who Jesus Christ was and therefore the Church is built on him, and everyone who makes the same discovery is another stone built in the edifice.

So Peter has discovered who Jesus is. Jesus then says, 'Don't tell anybody; at this stage tell no one.' Why? Because if they had told anyone they would have preached of the Messiah - his might and majesty and power - and there would have been a revolution on the spot. Palestine was like tinder. In the seventy years before Jesus there were seventeen rebellions in which 57,000 Jews were killed. Jesus knew quite well (after the feeding of the five thousand they tried to make him king) that Palestine then was like tinder. The disciples had first to be taught. They had to learn who the Messiah was before they could make it public.

So Jesus has discovered that there is at least one man who knows who he is. But there is something more. In an aeroplane journey there is a point which is called the point of no return. When you pass that point there is no going back: you must go on. Jesus came to this point - the point when he cannot turn back (he is going to Jerusalem). It must be all or nothing. He must go on now; he must be sure. If he is going to Jerusalem to die, he wants to be quite sure he is doing the right thing.

He goes to Mount Hermon with three of his disciples and there he has a vision. In the vision there come to him Moses and Elijah, the great law-giver and the great prophet, the two greatest people in the whole of Israel's history, and he talks to them about the death he is going to die. They say, 'Yes, we saw this long ago. Go on - you are right, you are on the right way.' And then something still bigger, out of a glistening cloud there comes a voice, which says, 'This is my Son, the beloved and the only one, listen to him.'

Jesus knows then that not only has he history on his side, but that God himself is telling him to go on. Thus once and for all the point of no return is passed - Jesus knows now that Peter has recognized him, that his country's history has culminated in him, that God approves of him. The stage is set for the last journey, for Jerusalem, and for the Cross.

4

TRAGEDY

In this world there are two kinds of courage. There is what might be called the courage of the moment, when a man with an almost instinctive reaction and almost without thinking reacts to some dangerous and menacing situation and becomes a hero almost before he has noticed it. And there is the courage of the man who can see the terrible and the threatening thing on the distant horizon and who could quite easily escape if he wished to do so and yet goes steadily, inflexibly on.

In Homer's *Iliad*, Achilles is told by his mother Thetis that if he goes out to the battle he will certainly die, and his answer is, 'Nevertheless I am for going on.' William Tyndale gave the Bible in English to the English people - the Church of his day did not want the common people to have the Scriptures and they burned his Bible. Tyndale said, 'I doubt not but they will burn me too, if it be God's will.' It was eight years before they burned him and eight years is a long time to wait for death, but Tyndale went steadily, inflexibly on.

There is no doubt at all which is the higher kind of courage: that of the man who sees on the distant horizon the terrible thing and who goes steadily and unswervingly on and who will not turn back.

That kind of courage was the courage of Jesus. It did not take divine foreknowledge to see the Cross. No special power of prophecy was needed to see what would happen when he went to Jerusalem; anyone who could read events at all knew that for Jesus to go to Jerusalem was to die.

Jesus on Trial
It would be impossible to exaggerate the horror and the shame and the humiliation of the last twelve hours of Jesus' life immediately preceding

CHRISTIAN MARTYRS

Who	When	Where	How
Stephen	1st cent AD	Jerusalem	Stoned
Perpetua and Felicitas	202	Carthage, N. Africa	Killed by wild beasts
Thomas Becket	1170	Canterbury, England	Stabbed
Thomas More	1535	London, England	Beheaded
William Tyndale	1536	Vilvorde, Belgium	Strangled and burned at the stake
Dietrich Bonhoeffer	1945	Flossenburg, Germany	Hanged
Martin Luther King Jr.	1968	Memphis, America	Shot
Bishop Janani Iuwum	1977	Kampala, Uganda	"Motor Accident"
Archbishop Oscar Romero	1980	San Salvador	Shot
Fr. Jerzy Popieluszko	1984	Wloclawek, Poland	Beaten and suffocated

his crucifixion. He was arrested in the garden, probably about nine o'clock in the evening. Between then and nine o'clock the next morning he underwent no fewer than six different trials. We have this not from any one gospel - we have to put the whole four gospels together and work out the pattern of the six. First of all he was taken immediately after his arrest to the house of Annas. Annas at this time held no office at all, but had been High Priest. But although not in office, Annas was the power behind the throne. Four of his sons had been High Priests and Caiaphas, the reigning High Priest, was his son-in-law.

Jesus was first brought to Annas for the very simple reason that Jesus had done something which touched Annas on the raw and Annas wanted to gloat over him. The point was this - in his cleansing of the Temple Jesus had driven from the Temple Court those who sold pigeons and doves. These were sold to the pilgrims who wanted to make sacrifices for sin, for thanksgiving, for peace, when they came to the Temple. Because every sacrifice that was offered had to be without spot and without blemish, and in order that it might be certain that the sacrifices *were* without spot or blemish, the Temple had appointed inspectors. Pilgrims could buy their victims, their pigeons and their doves, outside quite easily, but if they did buy them outside and then took them into the Temple and submitted them to the inspector, they could be quite, quite certain that he would find a flaw in them. When he found a flaw in them he would say, 'Don't you think you'd better buy your pigeon at our stalls? Our stalls have already been tested and you'll have no bother and no worry if you buy there.' Very well, and very convenient - except for this one thing, that outside the Temple on could buy two pigeons for 4 pence and inside the same two pigeons would cost 75 pence! These stalls where they sold the pigeons belonged to Annas. (They were actually called the bazaars of Annas.) Annas and his family made $70,000 a year out of them. Annas was glad then to get the chance to gloat over this upstart Galilean who had tried to hit his vested interest by cleansing the Temple in that way.

After Jesus had been examined - gloated over - by Annas, he was taken to the house of Caiaphas. But this investigation at the house of Caiaphas was not an official trial, or even a trial at all - this was an investigation to find a charge on which Jesus could be tired by the Sanhedrin. Through the night this unofficial thing lasted for hours, and the charge which they finally discovered was the charge of blasphemy. They were going to accuse Jesus of claiming to be the Son of God.

When morning came they took Jesus to the Sanhedrin. This was the supreme court of the Jews and, at least in religious matters, it had jurisdiction over every Jew throughout the world. Of course, at the time of which we are speaking, Palestine was an occupied country. The Sanhedrin had power therefore to pass the death sentence, but it had no power to carry the death sentence out. In order that the death sentence could be carried out, Jesus had to be taken next to the Roman governor, because only Pilate, representing the Roman government, had the power to carry out this sentence.

When we read the trial before Pilate, one thing is crystal clear, that Pilate was quite certain that Jesus was not guilty. Pilate wanted to let Jesus go and yet Pilate could not let him go - why? Quite simply, because Pilate was in a spot. His past rose up against him and made it impossible to do what he knew he ought to do. Pilate must have been a good governor and a wise administrator, because Judaea was one of the most difficult provinces in the Roman Empire and only a very efficient official would have been put in charge of it. But when he came to Judaea, Pilate got off on the wrong foot straight away.

What happened was this. The Roman troops were stationed, not in Jerusalem but in the Roman government headquarters at Caesarea, between twenty and thirty miles away; when troops were needed, when Jerusalem was crowded and there was a chance of trouble, detachments of them were brought from Caesarea and stationed temporarily in Jerusalem. Now a Roman soldier's standards were not flags like the standards of British regiments; they were poles with little metal busts of the Emperor on the top. The Emperor in those days was held to be divine, and so to the Jew the little metal bust on the top of the pole was a graven image, an idol, an image of a strange god. All Roman governors and commanders, up to the time of Pilate, had removed these little images before they marched their troops in, in deference to the religious feelings of the Jews. But Pilate said, 'Not on your life. I'm not taking away the figure of the Emperor for these Jews or anyone else.' And he marched in with the figure of the Emperor on the standards. There was no riot; the Jews simply besought Pilate with all their hearts to take away the image and not to desecrate the city. They followed him down to Caesarea and for five days they tagged on behind him in their hundreds, with their prayers and their requests. On the sixth day he said he would meet them in the amphitheatre and give them his answer. Some thousands of them were there, and his answer was that unless they stopped their requests on the spot, the soldiers who surrounded them would kill them in cold blood. The Jews simply bared their necks and said, 'Kill us, but don't desecrate our city.' Now even Pilate could not kill thousands in cold blood: he had to climb down.

But Pilate was curiously unteachable. He wanted to bring a water supply into Jerusalem and to build an aqueduct - an entirely laudable and praiseworthy undertaking. But aqueducts cost money. He had no money, and so raided the Temple treasury (which counted its money in nothing less than millions). Of course the Jews wanted water all right, but they did not want the Temple treasury raided - they went up in a blue light straight away and rioted. Pilate then dressed his troops in plain clothes, gave them cudgels beneath their cloaks, and sent them in among the crowds. Unless the riot stopped, at a given signal the soldiers were to do a bit of beating up. But something went badly wrong. Instead of just beating up, the soldiers got quite out of control and two thousand Jews lay dead in the streets of Jerusalem that night.

Pilate's whole trouble was this, that a Roman governor could be reported to the Emperor for mismanagement. In this the Jews had the whip hand of Pilate. They were saying, 'If you don't condemn this man you're not Caesar's friend.' In effect, they were saying, 'If you let this man go we are going to report you to Caesar, and you've had it.' And Pilate simply could to take the stand. But he still tried to shuffle out of the responsibility, even to the very last minute. He suddenly discovered that Jesus was a Galilean by original residence, and at that time there was present in Jerusalem, as Luke tells, the Herod who was King of Galilee, an area not under Pilate's jurisdiction. So Pilate took the chance and decided that the would send Jesus to Herod to see of Herod would take the responsibility of condemning him. But Herod would not. He simply examined him and sent him back to Pilate. So the sixth trial comes with Jesus back again before Pilate.

We can now list those six trials in the one night; first to Annas, then to Caiaphas; then to the Sanhedrin, then to Pilate, then to Herod, and then back to Pilate. One after another. And Jesus got no justice from

JESUS' LAST HOURS

Jesus is taken to:

Annas	–	–	–	John 18:13
Caiaphas	Matthew 26:57	Mark 14:53	Luke 22:54	John 18:24
Sanhedrin	Matthew 26:59	Mark 14:55	Luke 22:66	–
Pontius Pilate	Matthew 27:2	Mark 15:1	Luke 23:1	John 18:28
Herod	–	–	Luke 23:7	–
Pilate	–	–	Luke 23:11	–

Pilate because Pilate was afraid and wanted to keep his job rather than to give impartial Roman justice.

But Jesus had got less than justice long before he arrived before Pilate. Jesus had got much less than justice from the Jewish Sanhedrin. Now this Sanhedrin was a court whose whole procedure was designed to protect the person under trial - there never was a court in all history whose rules were so weighted in favour of the person being tried. The Sanhedrin was composed of seventy people with the ruling High Priest as the president over it. They sat in a semicircle so that every member could see every other member. When verdicts were given, they had to be given individually, beginning with the youngest member and moving on to the most senior. The youngest gave their verdict first lest they should be afraid to give their verdict after the older people had given it. All evidence had to be supported by the evidence of two witnesses examined independently. The person on trial could not be asked any question the answering of which was liable to incriminate him. And if the verdict after the examination was a verdict of death, it could not be carried out on the same day - a night had to elapse, so that the Sanhedrin might possibly change its mind and have mercy.

That is what the Sanhedrin *ought* to have done. But when we look at what the Sanhedrin *did* do, there is no question of independent verdicts. There is no question but that the High Priest asked Jesus an incriminating question when he said, 'Are you the Son of God?' - a question he had no right to ask. There is no question of a night elapsing between the verdict and the carrying out of the sentence; they rushed Jesus to death as quickly as they possibly could.

Again, we should not blame the Jews - we would have done exactly the same. In this the Jews are simply the representatives of mankind. Jesus was the great disturber, and since no one likes to be disturbed, they wanted to eliminate him as quickly as they possibly could. so Jesus was tried ... was condemned to death ... was led out to be crucified.

Suffering and Death

There is a certain line of thought which says that you should never linger on the physical suffering of Jesus - that in fact you should not speak of them at all. I differ from that; I think it is just being fastidious, or over-fastidious. I cannot forget that what Jesus suffered he suffered for me. I therefore think we must see what he actually did suffer.

When a man was condemned to this death, first of all he was scourged - tied to an X-like wooden frame in such a way that his back was bent so that he could not move, then thirty-nine lashes were laid on. The lash was a long leather thong, studded at intervals with sharpened bits of bone and pellets of lead, and it literally tore a man's back to shreds: few retained their consciousness, many went mad and not a few died. After that the person had to take upon his back the heavy crosspiece of his cross; Jesus staggered and fell under it. Put in the centre of a square of four Roman soldiers, he was taken in that way to the place of crucifixion by every possible street, square and avenue - the longest possible way - in order that people might see and be terrified at what happens to criminals. When they reached the place of crucifixion the cross was laid flat on the ground and the cross-piece fitted in. There was a little bit in the centre called the saddle which projected between the criminal's legs. Then the criminal was normally given a drink of drugged wine, prepared by some of the pious and kindly women of Jerusalem (Jesus would not take it: he would meet death a its ultimate worst, open-eyed and unafraid). Then he was laid on the cross, still flat on the ground; his hands were nailed; and then - just think of this moment - the cross was raised upright and put in the slot. The man was left to die. Jesus was lucky: he died at three o'clock in the afternoon. Criminals often hung for a week, dying slowly of hunger and thirst, going slowly mad.

An astonishing thing came at the end; Jesus said, 'Father, into thy hands I commend my spirit.' This was the first good-night prayer that every Jewish mother taught her little boy, just as some of us were probably taught, 'This night I lay me down to sleep ...' Jesus died with a child's prayer on his lips.

The Meaning of the Cross
We ask now, What happened on the Cross? On this I am quite definitely not arguing. I do not want to argue. You may think differently from me, you probably do.

To put it generally, there are two views of the Cross, one objective and one subjective, or one that thinks of the Cross as doing something to God, and the other that thinks of the Cross as doing something to man.

The first view of the Cross is just this - and I suppose it is the commonest view of the Cross - that on the Cross Jesus bore the agony, the pains and the penalty that we should have borne. The idea is that we were under the condemnation of God, and God was going to eliminate us, when Jesus came to God and said, 'Let me bear it for them.' Jesus is our substitute, bearing the punishment that we should have borne.

Brought up in that view, very early, while still a boy, I began to feel there was something quite desperately wrong with it. I thought there were two things wrong. First this, that it implies or actually says that something Jesus did changed the attitude of God, that God's hand was posed to strike, his condemnation poised to obliterate, and Jesus came and begged us off as it were, by taking it upon himself. Somehow or other Jesus changed a wrathful, angry God into a gentle God. I could always understand, even then, the saying of a little girl, 'Mummy, I love Jesus but I hate God.' And I went to the New Testament and I could

Via Dolorosa – Monastery of the Flagellation and Ecce Homo Arch

find no evidence for this at all, for the New Testament has nothing but God's love - 'God so loved the world that he sent his Son'. In Jesus God proves his *love*, that while we were yet enemies Christ died for us. The whole thing is inside the love of God. I saw this; I could not help seeing it. Jesus did not change the attitude of God; Jesus shows what the attitude of God is like. And then there was something else which came to me. It was supposed to be for the sake of his justice that God punished Jesus - to satisfy God's justice someone has to take the punishment, and that someone was Jesus. It came to me when I was still young that this means that in order to satisfy his justice, God had to do the unjustest thing this world has ever seen; that in order to satisfy his holy justice he punished the only perfectly good man there ever was, his own beloved Son. I began to feel I could not believe in a God like that or trust a God who did such a thing. For a while I was out of Christianity altogether, completely.

I began to think again and I came to that thing which is always in my mind - that in Jesus we see perfectly displayed the mind of God. This is God - in these last days, in that last week - this is God from beginning to end, saying 'I love you like that; you can batter me, you can bruise me, you can forsake me, you can crown me with thorns, you can treat me with injustice, you can scourge me - I love you, nothing will stop me loving you.' And this is why, in the end, Jesus had to die - because if Jesus had not died it would have meant that at some point the love of God said, 'Thus far and no further. Stop, I can't love you any more.'

Now no one ever thought of God like that, ever. Usually we think of God as the King, the Judge who is going to punish - no one ever thought of a God of love like that ... this immortal, indestructible lover - nobody. We know the story of the teacher who was teaching the lesson of the prodigal son - 'The son broke his father's heart ... went away to the far country ... behaved like ten kinds of fools, spent all his money ... came home; the father was watching for him ... the some came down the road and into the house - and what do you think the father will do to him?' Up went the hands - 'Well?' 'Bash him!' Well, of course that is the natural answer; that is exactly what we would expect the father to do. But no - not God; God loves, God loves.

Nothing will stop me loving you

I remember the story that A. J. Gossip used to tell, of the railway journey which George Adam Smith made. In the carriage was a Roman Catholic priest, a handsome young man. This priest was going out to a place in West Africa where at that time a white man's life was months, not years. George Adam Smith pleaded with the young man not to go; could he not find some other way of serving God - must he throw away his life like that? But the boy was adamant. He was travelling further, but George Adam Smith was getting out, and even at the carriage window George Adam Smith was still pleading. The train began to move away ... The priest took the silver crucifix from his belt and held it up, and he said, 'He loved me and gave himself for me, and I - can I hold back?' And when we are confronted with that immortal, indestructible love of the Cross, what else can we say?

> Where the whole realm of nature mine,
> That were an offering far too small,
> Love so amazing, so divine,
> Demands my life, my soul, my all.

5

TRIUMPH

It was nine o'clock on a Friday morning when Jesus was crucified, and at three o'clock in the afternoon he was dead. According to the first three Gospels, just before Jesus died he uttered a great shout, and the fourth Gospel tells us what that great shout was - 'It is finished.' (In Greek 'it is finished' is just one word, *tetelestai*). Jesus shouts *Finished!* This is not the cry of weary resignation or defeat, this is the shout of a man who has accomplished his task, whose work is done.

True or False?
A certain modern poet thinking of that, and thinking of the soldiers sitting gambling at the foot of the Cross for Jesus' clothes, wrote a poem like this:

> And sitting down they watched Him there,
> The soldiers did,
> And while they played with dice
> He made His sacrifice
> To rid God's world of sin.
>
> He was a gambler too, my Christ,
> He took His life and threw it for a world redeemed,
> And ere the westering sun went down
> Crowning that day with its golden crown,
> He knew that He had won.

True or false? Had he really won? Or was this simply the delusion of a man who was wiped out and eliminated and expunged from history? That is the question to ask now, when we speak about the Resurrection. There are some claims so great that if they are true nothing else in the world matters, and if they are not true, they are the biggest swindle that has ever been perpetrated on mankind. The Resurrection is like that. If the Resurrection is a fact, it is the most important single event in history. If the story of the Resurrection is not true, then it is the biggest delusion that has ever come across the mind of man.

I begin by quoting certain modern poets and then certain passages of the New Testament, and by asking a simple question. First of all I quote a poem by John Drinkwater:

Shakespeare is dust and will not come
To answer from his Avon tomb,
And Socrates and Shelley keep
An Attic and Italian sleep.

They see not, but, O Christians, who
Throng Holborn and Fifth Avenue,
May you not meet in spite of death
The traveller from Nazareth?

'May you not meet in spite of death the traveller from Nazareth?' True or false? Is this a fact of history or is this simply the deluded imagination of some poet? That is the question.

Again, I quote the poem by Francis Thompson:

But when (so sad thou canst not sadder)
Cry - and upon thy so sore loss
Shall shine the traffic of Jacob's ladder
Pitched betwixt Heaven and Charing Cross.
Yea, in the night, my Soul, my daughter,
Cry - clinging Heaven by the hems;
And lo, Christ walking on the water
Not of Gennesareth, but Thames!

'Christ walking on the water not of Gennesareth, but Thames' - true or false? Is it simply a poet's deluded dream, or is it a fact - which?

Now we go to the New Testament and we look at the last thing that Jesus is reported to have said before he left this world for good, in the body. Jesus said, 'Lo, I am with you always, even unto the end of the

The Garden Tombs

world.' True or false? Is this simply a deluded statement of someone who is altogether idealistically out of his mind? Or is it a fact?

Now take something on the other side. When Jesus was crucified, there was a centurion in charge of the crucifixion. That man watched Jesus dying and, when Jesus did die, this man was on his knees before

the Cross saying, 'Truly this man was a Son of God.' *Was?* Is this the word you're going to use of Jesus - truly this man *was* the Son of God? 'Was', or 'is'? Must you say of Jesus 'was', including him with all the figures of the past; someone who is dead and gone and *was?* Or must you say *'is'* - someone who is still present here and now? That is the question.

Arguments against the Resurrection

First we look at the claims that have been made against the Resurrection, the arguments that have been used to prove that the Resurrection never happened. One argument is that people say there are discrepancies in the stories in the various Gospels. They say, for instance, that the Resurrection appearances in Matthew happen in Galilee, but in Luke they happen in Jerusalem and its neighbourhood; in John the Resurrection appearances happen in Jerusalem and Galilee. Further, these people take up the question of the person at the tomb who gave the message. In Mark the person who gave the message at the tomb is 'one young man'. In Luke the message is given at the tomb by 'two young men in shining apparel' but in Matthew the person at the tomb is 'one angel' and in John it is 'two angels'. Now, they say, here we have discrepancy and differences and we cannot believe in narratives which have these discrepancies and differences among them.

We shall just think of it this way - there are discrepancies and differences, but these are all in the dramatic apparatus and outside events, and never in the central fact of the Resurrection of our Lord. Take a very modern analogy. Three men may go to a football match, and they will come home with entirely different stories. According to one, one team should have won; according to the other the other team should have won. According to one, so-and-so's a very dirty player; according to the other he's merely enthusiastic. According to one, there was a marvellous referee; according to the other he should have been hung. But the one thing that never changes in all the stories is the score - they can change the dramatic apparatus all right, but they can't alter the score. Now it's just so with the Resurrection - one can change the outside apparatus, change this event, that event, but the fact of the Resurrection never varies from beginning to end. Then take the case of our young man in Mark turning into two angels in John. Well, so what? Mark was written about the year 60, John about the year 100. If the most wonderful story in the world is told and retold for forty years, it is bound to acquire miraculous detail on the way through; this is only human nature. But the *fact* never varies from beginning to end.

Sir James Hope-Simpson, the famous banker, in a conversation about cheques and signatures on cheques, said that if you have two cheques which are supposed to have been signed by the same person, and hold these cheques up to the light and the two signatures coincide absolutely exactly, not a waving of the line, not a millimetre's departure, then you can be perfectly sure that one of them is a forgery, for no person ever signs his name in exactly the same way twice.

This is true. If a school teacher has two boys telling him exactly and precisely the same story, if a teacher at the University has two students flinging precisely the same story at him, then he can be quite sure that this is not the truth, this is collusion and collaboration. Stories are bound to differ when different people tell them, and the very discrepancies are the sign of truth. If the narratives of the Resurrection had been fiction, they would have been adjusted to fit - anyone in their senses would have adjusted them to fit. The very fact that they do not fit shows that fundamentally here we have people who are telling the truth as they know it.

No, the discrepancies need not worry us overmuch. On the other hand, there are some people who have tried to explain the Resurrection away altogether. First, there are those who say that Jesus did not die on the Cross but only fainted, and then he woke up, revived, in the tomb, and escaped. With this we must realize what a tomb was like. They did not bury people in the ground in those days. A tomb then looked like a cave. Looking in at the cave, we would see shelves, shelves on which, after they had wound it round in yards and yards and yards of grave clothes which were like bandages - strip after strip after strip - with perfume and ointment in between to embalm, the body was laid. This was all closed up not with a door but with a big, circular solid wheel which ran in a groove. Bigger than a cartwheel, it sometimes took as many as twenty men to move it. What are people saying when they say Jesus fainted and revived? He was scourged; he was crucified; the spear was thrust into his side and water and blood came out, the sign of a literally broken heart. He was put in the tomb and his body handled and those grave clothes were put round and round him; he was laid on the shelf. If he revived, how on earth did he get out of the grave clothes?

How on earth did he get out of the tomb? And if he did emerge, why was he not a broken, battered, bruised figure - instead of someone vital with life? That theory really won't wash!

A second suggestion is that the Jews stole away Jesus' body because they were afraid that his tomb would become a martyr's monument and that people would go there to worship his body. Just think what is being said! There is not a single Christian sermon in the whole book of Acts which is not based on the Resurrection - all that the Jews had to do was to produce the body and Christianity would have been blown sky-high. If the Jews had snatched the body, they would certainly have said so without any hesitation.

It is said that it was not the Jews who removed the body - that it was the disciples who removed it and then said that Jesus had risen from the dead. Again, just think what is being said! By AD70 every one of the disciples was dead with the exception of John, and every one had died a violent, agonizing death - on the cross or in the flames or by the wild beasts. But if one carries out a swindle one does it for profit - not for blood and sweat and tears. Men have died for a delusion, but men have never died for what they *know* was a downright lie for which they were responsible. Again, this theory won't work.

People have suggested that the Resurrection stories are really the product of hallucination, that the disciples did believe that Jesus had risen from the dead, but it was just an hallucination. Just think what is being said! I suppose it is possible that one man should have an hallucination and that even two men should have an hallucination, but Paul says that one of the resurrection appearances was to more than five hundred Christians all at the one time, of whom many are still alive! (Paul would like to add, 'If you like, go and ask them.') Now it is quite incredible that five hundred people should all have the one hallucination and all at the same time; that is just beyond belief altogether.

Now there is a kind of 'sub' theory here, and that is that belief in the Resurrection grew up through a kind of self-hypnotism. This idea is specially connected with Peter. The idea is that Peter said to himself, 'Jesus can't be dead, Jesus must be alive; Jesus was so wonderful, so brave, so powerful, death can't have touched him. He must be alive.'

And all of a sudden Peter moved from saying 'He must be alive' to 'He *is* alive', and hypnotized himself into saying it. This we might believe, if we left an interval of years for it to work - but the Resurrection happened just two days after the burial. One cannot imagine this happening, as it were, overnight. And again, even if this happened to Peter, it does not explain why hundreds of people began to believe in the Resurrection, all arriving at it in their own way. Again, this won't work.

And then there is what is the strangest of all explanations of the Resurrection. It is said, by a certain critic, that the story of the Resurrection goes back to a hysterical and tear-blinded woman. This idea was once suggested like this: Mary Magdalene went to the garden to find the tomb, to weep and to worship. She could not find the tomb and she met a young man and she told him she was looking for Jesus' tomb, and the young man said to her, 'He is not here, look, there is where they buried him.' According to this, the sentence 'He is risen' is a later addition. So this young man said 'He is not here, look, there is where they buried him.' This story goes on to say that Mary, blinded by her tears, went to the wrong tomb, and having gone to the wrong tomb she found it empty and went back and said that Jesus had risen from the dead. Well, if you can believe that you can believe anything! If true, it means that no one checked this story at all, and that no one went to see, which is unbelievable.

Something Happened - Something Spiritual
No, I don't think you can really take these objections to the Resurrection seriously. I don't think these objections compel us for one moment to abandon our belief. I wish I could stop there, but I cannot. There is much more to be said than that. The story is not nearly so simple as it is if you just left it there. When you read the Resurrection narratives there is one thing that stands out a mile. It is just this: *Jesus never appeared to anyone except to those who loved him.* He always appeared to those who were thinking about him and speaking of him. Two men are going along the road to Emmaus, they are loving Jesus, they are thinking about him, they are in despair - and there he is. His disciples are in the upper room and they are sorrowing for him and they

JESUS' RESURRECTION APPEARANCES

Jesus meets the lady at the tomb	Matthew 28:9
Jesus meets eleven disciples-the Great Commission	Matthew 28:18
Jesus appears to Mary Magdalene	Mark 16:9*
Jesus appears to two others	Mark 16:12*
Jesus appears to the eleven- the Great Commission	Mark 16:14*
Jesus meets two on the Emmaus road Luke 24:15	
Jesus appears to the eleven and others Luke 24:36	
Jesus appears to Mary Magdalene	John 20:14
Jesus appears to the disciples	John 20:19
Jesus appears again to the disciples (incl. Thomas)	John 20:26
Jesus appears to the disciples by Lake Galilee	John 21:1
Luke, in Acts, reports resurrection appearances	Acts 1:3
Paul reports resurrection appearances	1 Corinthians 15:5-7

(*Mark 16:9-20 does not appear in early manuscripts)

are loving him - there he is. He appeared *only* to those who loved him. But if you and I had been writing a fictional novel about the Resurrection, who would we have made Jesus appear to? I think certainly we would have made him appear to Annas and to Caiaphas and to Pilate. He would have burst into the room, towered over them in glory and said, 'You have tried to crucify me, but here I am' - what a dramatic confrontation! It never happens, never.

It is only to those who loved him - only to those who are talking about him; only to those who are longing for him; only to those in whose hearts and minds he is there *all* the time, that he appears. Clearly there is a subjective element in this. This is to say, we shall never see the risen Lord unless there is love for the risen Lord inside us; we have to bring this with us before we can see the risen Lord. Now this seems to me to prove that we are working not in the realm of the earthly and the physical and the material, but in that of the spiritual.

We must move on and come to the greatest evidence of the Resurrection of all, and that is not in any of the gospels, but in 1 Corinthians, chapter 15. Now 1 Corinthians 15 was written at least ten years earlier than any of the Gospels, and this chapter tells of Paul's personal experience. This is Paul telling us what happened to him. He tells how Jesus appeared to Peter, and Jesus appeared to James, and Jesus appeared to more than five hundred Christians at the one time, and Jesus appeared to the twelve, and Jesus appeared to all the apostles - and then he says, 'and as to one untimely born, he appeared to me'.

Now if there is one thing quite certain it is that Paul is putting Jesus' appearance to him on a level with all the other appearances. This is the whole point - the appearance to Peter, the appearance to James, the appearance to the five hundred, the appearance to Paul - they are all exactly the same, the same appearance of the same risen Christ. Yes, but the appearance to Paul was no less than three years after all the others. And certainly the appearance to Paul was no physical, material thing; it was obviously a spiritual appearance, a vision - a personal appearance to Paul, nobody seeing anything, perhaps not even Paul himself, just a blinding, blazing light. Now this seems to me to prove that we are working and walking in a realm of the spirit and not in the realm of physical and material things at all. Even when we read the gospels we get hints of this. In the gospels people are walking to Emmaus, suddenly Jesus is there; the disciples are in the upper room, the door locked - Jesus is there, in the midst of them. Now clearly this is not physical and material and earthly, this is spiritual. This is spirit meeting with spirit and, when we come to this, something happens, something really happens. We are not talking about earthly and bodily things, we are talking about spiritual things which can yet happen.

My own experience with the Resurrection stories was that for a long time they meant nothing to me. My reaction to this story of Jesus who came back and in flesh and blood walked about this world for seven weeks and then ascended up on high was - well, so what? What has this got to do with me? Is he here still? And then I came to see that in this there is not just flesh and blood, but spirit; and that just as Jesus walked with Paul and with Peter, he can walk with me - because this is not physical but spiritual reality. And the older I get the more I think that I believe two things about the Resurrection.

First I believe unquestionably that *something happened* - the whole existence of the Church depends on the Resurrection; without the Resurrection we cannot explain the Church. There are the disciples just after the Crucifixion, men who are in utter and complete despair. Their hearts are broken; their minds are absolutely desolated. Devastated, they are in the upper room. The door is locked; they are in terror - listening to every step on the stair - waiting for a rap at the door, when it would be their turn next. Cowards - without a speck of courage or anything else! And then seven weeks pass, just seven weeks, and it is Pentecost, and this Peter, who had been shuddering with terror behind a locked door, is preaching Jesus Christ to that mob in Jerusalem. A few days later he is arrested and brought before the Sanhedrin, the very same court which condemned his Lord to death. And there, as brave as a lion, he is saying, 'Whether it be right to obey God or you, *you* decide - we are obeying God.' Taking his life in his hands - the coward has become the hero. We must explain this.

Every effect has got to have an adequate cause and the only way you can explain this miraculous (and I use the word advisedly) change in the disciples is that they were convinced that Jesus was still alive. Something had happened to them which convinced them, once, finally, and for all that Jesus was still living. They were sure that their living Lord was with them. As I see it, the simple fact is this - apart from the Resurrection there would have been no Church; apart from the Resurrection you and I would never have heard the name of Jesus Christ, because the disciples would just have gone away and tried to forget. So in the first place I am utterly convinced that something happened.

But in the second place I am equally convinced that *I do not know exactly and precisely what happened.* What I am sure of is that I am not moving in a physical, earthly flesh-and-blood world, but in a world of the spirit. And because I am moving in a world of the spirit I am not believing in a man who walked about for seven weeks and then left. I am believing in someone who is still here with me at this very moment, now.

The Living Christ

I have told before the story that my old teacher A. J. Gossip used to love to tell. There was a week when he was so busy that he had hardly time to do anything, and he could only knock a sermon together just as quickly as possible. It was not much of a thing, but it was the best he could do. He was minister of St Matthew's Church, Glasgow, and he tells us that he was coming up the pulpit stair and as he came to the bend he met Christ. Christ said to him, 'Gossip, is this the best that you can do?', and under the circumstances of the week Gossip said, 'Lord, it is.' And Jesus took that sermon that night and it was a trumpet to call men to God. I quite believe that. I believe that implicitly, that it happened and that it took place.

I am not interested in a man who became flesh and blood for seven weeks and then went back to Heaven. I am interested in that spiritual Christ whose life the disciples were perfectly certain went on. I am interested in that Christ because I am perfectly certain that he is here now, this minute, and that at any time I can claim and receive the strength and the comfort which he alone can give.

6

HIS BODY THE CHURCH

If you are going to join any association whatsoever, you are always better to know just exactly what you are joining. Before you join any club or institution you want to know just what you can expect and just what is expected of you. What is true of any association or group or club is true of the Church. If you want to become a member of the Church or if you want to consider the Church, it is only right to know what the Church is and what it stands for and what are its duties and its obligations and its privileges.

The Church is People
Now the Greek word for 'Church' is *ekklesia*, the word from which we get such words as 'ecclesiastical' and so on. The very use of this word gives us a very good insight into some definition of the Church. This word *ekklesia* has a double background. First of all, it has a Jewish background. When we read in the Old Testament, especially in books like Exodus and Numbers, the story of the journey of the children of Israel across the wilderness, every now and again we have the children of Israel assembled to listen to Moses - or rather to listen to some word of God which God had sent them through Moses - and when they are gathered like that the Authorized Version regularly talks of the 'congregation of Israel'. Now the word for 'congregation' in the Greek Old Testament is this word *ekklesia*. So first and foremost this word *ekklesia* describes a group of people who are listening for a word from God.

But Christianity very soon went out of Palestine and came into the Greek world, where this word *ekklesia* had a quite different meaning. In the Greek world *ekklesia* was not a religious word at all, but a political one. The *ekklesia* of a Greek city was the governing body of the city.

Now the Greeks had what seems to us the oddest form of government; they had the only true democracy there ever was. The governing body of a city like Athens was in fact every single citizen who possessed the vote; they all constituted the *ekklesia*. This meant the equivalent of government by a committee of twenty three thousand people, which is quite a committee. Now obviously all the people on this committee did not turn up at the one time. What happened was this. The *ekklesia* met twelve times in the year and before it was due to meet a herald went through the city saying, 'The *ekklesia* will meet at such and such a time, and in such and such a place, and you are requested to be present.' An *ekklesia* actually and in fact consisted of those who accepted the invitation to be present.

This gives us our second definition of the Church. The Church is composed of those people who have accepted the invitation of Jesus Christ to take him as Master and Lord.

So we have our double definition of the Church. The Church is a group of people who are listening for a word from God. The Church is a group of people who have accepted the invitation of Jesus Christ to take him as Master and Lord. But no sooner have we said that than we see at once a truth that stands out a mile. This means that *the Church is people!* You can read the New Testament from end to end and you will never find that the word 'church' describes a building - 'church' always describes people. In the days of the early Church they had no buildings - there was no such thing as a church building until well after AD200. They did all their preaching on the street, and they met in the rooms of people who had slightly larger houses. The word 'church' never even threatened to mean a building - it was always 'people'!

What is a Christian?

If the Church is people, then obviously the best way to find out what the Church is will be to look at the words for 'the Christian' in the New Testament and to see what these words are. Clearly we cannot look at anything like all the words, but we can look at one or two.

The first word we look at is the word which the Authorized Version usually translates 'saints' - Paul writes his letters to the saints of Ephesus, the saints of Rome, the saints at Corinth, and so on. Unfortunately this is rather a bad translation, because the word 'saint' suggests to us a kind of plaster image, or someone in a stained-glass window. We have only to read the Letters to the Corinthians to see that the Corinthian church was just as big a bother to Paul as any church is to its minister today. They were no more saintly, in that sense of the word, than we are now. But the word which is translated 'saint' is this word *hagios*, the word which is also much oftener translated 'holy'. And this word 'holy', whenever we meet it in the Bible, has a special meaning. It always has basically the meaning of *different*. Remember the Sabbath day to keep it holy - remember the Sabbath day to keep it different; the Temple is holy because it is *different* from other places; the Scripture itself is holy because it is different from other books. So then, first of all, when the Christian is called a saint, it means that he is different; the Christian is bound to be different.

Now in what sense is the Christian different? Well, there is a phrase that Paul uses over and over again, the phrase 'in Christ'. He uses it almost eighty times in his letters. The Christian is different in that his life is lived 'in Christ'. What does this mean? Many great New Testament scholars put it this way. If you are 'in Christ' it is like being 'in the atmosphere' - unless you are in the air and the air is in you, you die; and unless you are in Christ and Christ is in you, your spiritual life dies. If you are 'in Christ' it means Christ is the atmosphere in which you live - you never forget the presence of Jesus Christ - you always remember he is with you. You never want to do anything without saying to him, 'Lord, what do you want me to do?' All life is lived in his presence and in the awareness that he is there with you. This is the difference.

Now the point of this difference is that it has to be carried out in the ordinary everyday life that we live - it is not a difference which involves withdrawing from the world; it is a difference which must be lived out *in* the world. Jesus prayed to God and said, 'I do not pray that you should take them out of the world ... I pray that you should keep them from the sin of the world.'

Christians have not always seen this by any means. Some have thought that to be a Christian one must get right out of the world and leave the world alone. There were, for example, two kinds of people who sound fantastic to us nowadays. One was what were called the 'pillar saints'. These built themselves a pillar, and on top of it a little platform, where they lived. Even more fantastic were the people who were called *inclusi* - which means the shut-ups. They chose a niche, usually in some church, and they got into this niche and then had a brick wall built in front of the niche with only a slit left for people to push food through to them and for air to breathe. They thought this was being Christian - and, of course, one is safe from a whole lot of temptations put out of reach by being shut up in a pillar-box like that. But Christianity never meant this - it never meant withdrawing from the world like that.

People still need to learn the lesson. I knew a girl converted at an Evangelical campaign. Up to that time she had worked in the office of a great daily newspaper - and no one can call a daily newspaper a particularly religious institution. When she was converted she left the paper on the spot and entered the service of a religious paper where every word was religious, every person on the staff was religious, and even when they wanted a typist they advertised for a Christian typist, whatever that may be. However, this was precisely the opposite of what she should have done. She had run away. But the point is that a Christian is involved in life - the Christian ought to be involved in politics; he ought to be involved in local government. He ought to be involved in Parliament; he ought definitely to be involved in his Trade Union; he ought to be showing his Christianity right there where he is, on the spot, just exactly where he lives and moves and has his being.

Saints, Disciples, Believers
First of all there is this word *hagios* - saint, different. The second word I would look at is the word 'disciple'. The word 'disciple' literally means '*a learner*'. So the Christian ought to be a learner - a learner from the day of his entry into the Church until his death. What happened in the early Church was this. I said they preached on the street. Peter or Paul would be preaching and the pagans would be going by, and some of them would stop to listen. If they were not interested, of course they

just drifted on, but if they were interested they would stop and listen. If they were very interested they would go up to the preacher and they would say, 'Where can I find out more about this Jesus?' They would then be directed to one of the house churches, where they would be told more.

This ought to be the motive of the Christian from start to finish - 'Where do I find out more about Jesus?' - with the illimitable, unsearchable riches of God in front of him he must be learning all the time. The tragic thing is that so many Christians are the very opposite and are proud of it. They say, 'I've still got the simple faith I had when I was sixteen.' They refuse absolutely to grow, refusing everything that scholarship and knowledge and study and devotion can give to them. Their attitude stems from a wrong idea of conversion.

An awful lot of people think of conversion as the end of the road. They think when they're converted, 'That's me finished', that now they are fully fledged and perfect Christians. Just think what the word 'conversion' means. It comes from the Latin word *convertere*, which means to turn round. Conversion is a turning round, and when you turn round you face God instead of facing yourself. But there is no point in turning round and then standing stock-still. A steam locomotive, put on the turntable and turned, has not finished the journey it is being prepared for. So with the Christian - the Christian has to go steadily onwards each day, in study, in prayer, in self-discipline, learning more and more about the illimitable riches of God.

We have looked at *the saints*, the different ones; *the disciples*, the learners; and then we have *the believers*. This is quite a common title for the Christian in the New Testament, and it describes him as a person who has certain convinced beliefs. James Agate, the great dramatic critic, once said, 'My mind is not a bed to be made and remade. There are certain things on which I've made up my mind and I don't propose to change them.' The Christian is like that. He says, 'I believe'. But we can use this word 'I believe' in far more than one sense.

A certain psychologist put it this way. You can take three people and ask them the same question - the question is Do you believe in love?'

You go to a boy of eleven years of age and you ask him, 'Do you believe in love?' Oh yes,' he says, 'I believe in love. My big sister's in love and I can't get into the living room to see the television for her and her boy there every night! Of course I believe in love.' Then you go to a psychologist and you ask him, 'Do you believe in love?' The psychologist says, 'Oh yes, I believe in love because love is an emotional condition which has certain physical and mental reactions responding to certain stimuli - of course I believe in love.' Then you go to a couple walking home hand-in-hand under the stars after an evening out and you ask them, 'Do you believe in love?' They say, 'Don't be silly, we're *in* love!'

So we have three kinds of answer to 'Do you believe in love?' - from an external witness, from some kind of proof or from experience. Of course, the real belief in love is the Christian experience; the real belief in love in the experience of Jesus Christ. The Christian never says, 'I know *what* I have believed.' The Christian says, 'I know *whom* I have believed.' The Christian conviction is a conviction of the personal presence and fellowship of Jesus Christ.

The Body of Christ

So, then, a Christian is a *saint*, the one who is different, the *disciple*, the learner, the *believer*, the one who believes certain things. But the great title of the Christian is in the great title for the Church - *the Body of Christ*. This title is a one-word theology of the Church; it tells us almost everything about the Church.

The first thing it tells of is obviously the unity of the Church. A body is a unity; it is made of all kinds of different parts, but unless they are working harmoniously there is illness - everything must be doing its work, none must be doing too much work, they must all be just doing their own work and then health comes.

St Paul was not the first person to strike on this idea of the body as the picture of unity; it is in Livy, the Roman historian. There was a time when there was a split in Rome between the *plebs*, the common people, and the patricians, the aristocrats, and the split was so bad that the *plebs* walked out. Of course, when the *plebs* walked out in their thousands,

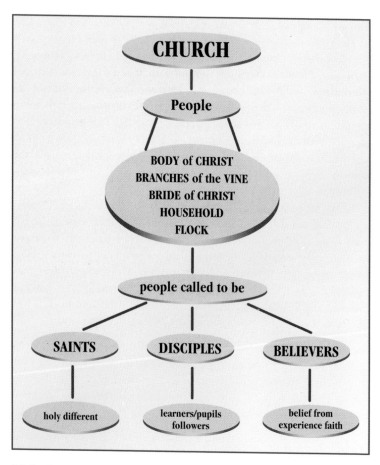

life in the city came to an end. So the patricians hired an orator called Menenius Agrippa and they told him to go out and try to bring the *plebs* back. He went out, but he did not make a speech and he gave them no row - he told them a story. He said, there was a time when the other members of the body got very angry in the stomach; they said, 'Here we work as hard as we can and there the stomach sits and does nothing, taking everything in that we bring to it.' And so - to use a very mixed metaphor - they decided to bring the stomach to heel: the hands decided that they would not lift the food to the mouth and the mouth decided it would not chew it, and the teeth decided they would not bite it and the tongue decided it would not taste it and the throat decided it would not swallow it. They said, 'We'll soon settle the stomach this way.' But instead they nearly brought death and destruction to the whole body by starvation. They then began to see that we must live in a unity, all things working together.

But this unity does not mean that there will be no arguments, that there will be no differences; it does not mean that at all. It will mean that there are most acute differences, but there is an over-arching love. I once knew a man who had been a minister of a church for forty-seven years and he said that in that forty-seven years he had never had a vote or discord in his Kirk Session.[1] That's peace, but it's the peace of death. Now I had only one congregation in my life, down in Renfrew, and that congregation taught me very much more than I ever taught it. At that time I think I had the most explosive and volcanic Kirk Session in Scotland. As a very young minister, I used to visualize the end of the evening coming with me holding their jackets, and I used to get quite worried about this, but then I began to notice something - that the men who had been arguing most violently with each other went up the road arm-in-arm afterwards in perfect friendship. There was one man called John Thomson, a fine man he was, who used to ring me up after one of these 'donnybrooks' (or Kirk Session Meetings) and say, 'That was a wonderful night we had tonight, wasn't it, Mr Barclay?' And I began to see that here I was oddly enough learning what Christian love was - I was learning that Christian love is that which over-arches all the differences.

Sir James Barrie, the playwright, was very close to his producer, Charles Frohman, and he used to say, 'I like Charlie very much indeed - I've only had one argument with Charlie in all my life and it lasted for eighteen years.' I know exactly what he meant. I teach in this University and I find that at the end of the day I am usually closest to the students who are furthest from me theologically. I know certain students think I probably ought to be muzzled, but in spite of that I am closer to them at the end of the day than anyone else. Their love over-arches the differences and this is what Christian unity is - not by any means a flat conformity, but the difference is included in the greater love.

If we think of Christianity, the Church, as the Body of Christ, this unity is a unity which exists in a difference at the same time. To take an analogy of this - a crowd of people want to sing; now the first thing they do is they decide they will all sing different tunes (and that may be a noise, but it is not a joyful noise); they quickly see there is no future in that, so they decide they will all sing the same tune, singing in unison. That is better, but it is not the highest kind of singing. But they then divide themselves into sopranos, contraltos, tenors and basses, and if they are very ambitious they get an orchestra, which may be playing as many as twenty different parts. So we may have twenty or thirty different parts all interwoven in this harmony, all singing together, but each man singing his own line. Now this is the Christian unity, unity in difference.

The older I get the more I begin to see that there are so many things which are neither right nor wrong. Some people like a very plain church; other people like an ornate cathedral. Some people like prayers which are just delivered in ordinary simple language; other people like an elaborate liturgy. There is no right or wrong about this; it is what brings us to God. But we will insist on sticking labels on people: Conservative, Radical, Liberal, Fundamentalist, and so forth ... and the minute we stick a label on a chap we put a wall between us and him. But the City of God is not like this.

There is a picture of the City of God in the book of the Revelation and in this City of God the walls are 12,000 furlongs long. Now 12,000 furlongs is 1,500 miles. A city whose walls are 1,500 miles square has an area of 2,250,000 square miles. This picture surely says, 'There's an awful lot of room in the Kingdom of God.' It's very different from the kind of reaction which you get in the four lines of doggerel:

We are God's chosen few,
All others will be damned;
There is no room in heaven for you,

We can't have heaven crammed.

There are people who speak exactly like that. But in God's Heaven there is a tremendous amount of room for everybody, and the differences are subsumed in this unity which is in God and which is under God all the time.

The Body at Work

The most important thing about this idea of the Church as the Body of Christ lies in this fact; when we speak of the Church as the Body of Christ, there is a sense in which we mean this absolutely literally.

Jesus is not here in the flesh now. He is here in the Spirit. And this means that if Jesus wants a job done, he has got to get a man or a woman to do that job for him. Here is a child and Jesus wants that child taught, but nothing will teach that child unless a man or a woman will do it. No amount of prayer will teach the child, you must go and do it. Here is an old body and Jesus wants this person consoled and comforted - nothing will do it unless someone will go and see her.

We hear a great many sermons about the might and the majesty and the power of God; we would be well sometimes to think of the helplessness of God, that without us and without what we can do God is quite and totally helpless. He has got to get a man! We are the Body of Christ, literally hands to do his work, feet to run upon his errands, a voice to speak for him. This is the Church's task; to be the body, the hands, the feet, through whom Christ acts. But so often the Church fails in this task.

Toscanini, the famous conductor, was once conducting an orchestra, and it was obvious that the orchestra was bored and was not trying. After struggling along for a while Toscanini laid down his baton and leant over the rostrum. 'Gentlemen,' he said, 'God has told me how he wants this symphony played and you - you hinder God.' So often the Church has done that.

One tremendous instance of that happened in 1271. Nicolo and Maffeo Polo were at the court of Kublai Khan, whose empire stretched from the Urals to the Himalayas, and from the Danube to the China Sea, and Kublai Khan said, 'I want you to go back to the Pope and I

PARTS OF THE BODY

One Spirit, Different Gifts (1 Cor. 12:8-10)	One Body, Different Parts (1 Cor 12:28)
wisdom	apostles
knowledge	prophets
faith	teachers
healing	miracle workers
miraculous powers	healers
prophecy	helpers
discernment of spirits	administrators
speaking in tongues	speakers in tongues
interpretation of tongues	

want you to ask him to send a hundred missionaries, and I'll become a Christian and all my great men will become Christians, and all my country will become Christians, and you will have more Christians in the east here than ever in the west.' So they went back and they asked the Pope, but the Pope was too busy playing politics. For eighteen years nothing was done and then a few missionaries were sent, just a handful; too late and too few. Now think what might have happened if that chance had been taken. China would have been Christian; Japan would have been Christian; the Middle East would have been Christian; Turkey would have been Christian, even India would have been Christian - the face of the world would have been changed. But the Church refused the chance.

There is a poem by George Eliot in which she depicts the famous maker of violins, Antonio Stradivari, speaking:

When any master holds
    'Twixt chin and hand a violin of mine,
He will be glad that Stradivari lived,

Made violins, and made them of the best.
　　... while God gives them skill
I give them instruments to play upon,
　　... if my hand slacked
I should rob God - since He is fullest good -
Leaving a blank instead of violins.
　　... 'Tis God gives skill,
But not without men's hand: He could not make
Antonio Stradivari's violins
Without Antonio.

'If my hand slacked I should rob God.' We have been thinking about the love, the sacrifice, the heroism, the generosity of Jesus Christ. Is all that go for nothing? That depends on you and me. For we are the Body of Christ.

[1] Known to others as the Parochial Church Council, or the Vestry.

JESUS - KEY EVENTS

Events in Jesus' life, as related in the Gospels.

	Matthew	Mark	Luke	John
Jesus' birth	1:18-25	–	2:1-7	–
Presentation in the temple	–	–	2:21-40	–
Baptism by John	3:13-17	1:9-11	3:21-22	–
Temptation in the wilderness	4:1-11	1:12-13	4:1-13	–
First miracle at Cana	–	–	–	2:1-11
The Beatitudes	5:1-12	–	6:17-26	–
Parables about the Kingdom	13:1-52	4:1-34	13:16-21	–
Jesus feeds the five thousand	14:13-21	6:30-44	9:10-17	6:1-13
Peter recognizes the Christ	16:13-20	8:17-30	9:18-22	–
Jesus' Transfiguration	17:1-13	9:2-13	9:28-36	–
Jesus' entry into Jerusalem	21:1-11	11:1-11	19:28-44	12:12-19
Jesus' arrest	26:47-56	14:43-52	22:47-53	18:1-11
Jesus' Crucifixion	27:32-44	15:21-32	23:26-43	19:17-27
Resurrection appearances	28:9; 16-20	16:9-18	24:13-49	20:10-21:25
Jesus' Ascension	–	16:19	24:50-53	–

Also available in this series . . .

Barclay's Life of Jesus

from John Hunt Publishing and Westminster John Knox Press. A chapter from this book is reprinted below.

WAITING FOR THE CALL

Even when a man discovers the task for which God has sent him into the world, he has still another problem to solve, the problem of when to begin upon it. If he begins too soon, he will begin without the necessary preparation and equipment for the task. If he waits until too late, he may never begin at all. If he chooses the wrong moment, his work may be foredoomed to failure even before he begins.

In the Temple Jesus had realized the futility of human ways of seeking for God, and he had made the great discovery that he had been sent into the world to bring all men to God; and now he had to await the call from God to set out upon his work. And Jesus waited long. He was twelve when the revelation in the Temple came to him (Luke 2.42); he was thirty when he left Nazareth to begin upon his work (Luke 3.23). Eighteen years is a long time to wait; but the silent years were not the wasted years, for they were years of preparation for the task that no one else in the world could do. Throughout the years Jesus was learning all the time.

He was learning the basic knowledge and the basic skills which are every man's equipment for life. As Luke tells us, he increased in wisdom and stature (Luke 2.52). He learned to read, for we know that the day was to come when he was to read the lesson from the prophets in the synagogue in Nazareth (Luke 4.16). He learned to write, which in those days was a much rarer accomplishment. In the story of the woman taken in adultery, we are told that Jesus stooped down and wrote on the ground (John 8.8). In that passage an

Armenian manuscript dating to AD 989 makes the curious addition that it was the sins of the woman's accusers which Jesus wrote on the ground, and that is why they slipped silently away. 'He himself, bowing his head, was writing with his finger on the earth, to declare their sins; and they were seeing their several sins on the stones.' Jesus was learning the skills which every boy must learn. There was a village school in Nazareth; to that village school Jesus must have gone. In that village school there was a nameless village schoolmaster, whose name no man will ever know, and yet that schoolmaster taught the Son of God. Many a teacher is doing a work far greater than he knows.

He was learning to do a good day's work, for it was as the carpenter of Nazareth that men knew him (Mark 6.3). Jesus was the good craftsman. Justin Martyr tells us: 'He was in the habit of working as a carpenter when he was among men, making ploughs and yokes', and there is a legend that Jesus of Nazareth made the best ox-yokes in all Galilee, and that men came from far and near to buy the yokes that Jesus made. Then as now craftsmen hung their trade sign and their slogan above their shops. Once Jesus said: 'my yoke is easy' (Matt. 11.30). The Greek word for *easy* is *chrestos*, which means *well-fitting*, and some one has imagined that the sign above the door of the carpenter's shop in Nazareth was an ox-yoke with the words painted on it: 'My yokes fit well.'

It is, indeed, significant to note what the New Testament actually calls Jesus; it calls him a *tekton* (Mark 6.3). A *tekton* was more than a carpenter; he was a craftsman who could build a wall or a house, construct a boat, or make a table or a chair, or throw a bridge across a little stream. In the old days—and even now in the country places—there were men who, with the craftsman's inborn skill, could turn their hands to any job. In their hands wood and metal and stones become obedient, and such was Jesus. William Soutar, the Scots poet, wrote a poem about the craftsman's hands of Jesus:

> Glaidly he dressed the rochest deal
> To mak a kist or door;
> Strauchtly he drave the langest nail
> Wi' little sturt or stour.

Monie a man as he gaed by,
And monie a kintra wench,
Wad watch the strang and souple hands
That wrocht abune the bench.

And aye sae true, sae tenderly,
Sae trysted wud they move
As they had been a lover's hands
That blindly kent their love.

In Nazareth Jesus got to himself the craftsman's strong and gentle hands.

He was winning the physical manhood to enable him to do his task. The time was to come when Jesus was to walk the roads of Palestine, and when he was to tell a would-be follower that the foxes had their holes and the birds of the air their nests, but that he had nowhere to lay his head (Luke 9.58). Jesus could never have lived the life he did live had he not been physically equipped for it. In those days a carpenter did not buy his wood from the saw-mill or from the wholesaler. He went out to the hill-side, chose his young tree, swung his axe, cut it down and carried it home on his shoulder. Certainly Jesus was no weak and anaemic person; he must have been bronzed and weather-beaten, in the perfection of physical manhood.

One of the great gaps in our knowledge of Jesus is that we do not know what in physical appearance he was like. In regard to this, tradition was divided into two. One line of thought began with Isaiah's picture of the Suffering Servant. 'His appearance was so marred, beyond human semblance' (Isa. 52.14). 'He had no form nor comeliness that we should look at him, and no beauty that we should desire him' (Isa. 53.2). Arguing from this, Irenaeus said that Jesus was weak, inglorious and without grace. Origen said he was small, ill-favored, and insignificant. Cyril of Alexandria even went the length of saying that he was 'the ugliest of the children of men'. The other line of thought stemmed from Ps. 45.2: 'You are the fairest of the sons of men.' This line of thought painted Jesus in words and in pictures in the beauty of the Olympian gods.

The most famous of all descriptions is in the *Letter of Lentulus*, who purports to be governor of Jerusalem:

> There has appeared here in our time, and still lives here, a man of great power named Jesus Christ. The people call him a prophet of truth, and his disciples the Son of God. He raises the dead and cures the sick. He is in stature a man of middle height and well proportioned. He has a venerable face, of a sort to arouse both fear and love in those who see him. His hair is the colour of ripe chestnuts, smooth almost to the ears, but above them waving and curling, with a slightly bluish radiance, and it flows over his shoulders. It is parted in the middle on the top of his head, after the fashion of the people of Nazareth. His brow is smooth and very calm, with a face without wrinkle or blemish, lightly tinged with red. His nose and mouth are faultless. His beard is luxuriant and unclipped, of the same colour as his hair, not long but parted at the chin. His eyes are expressive and brilliant. He is terrible in reproof, sweet and gentle in admonition, cheerful without ceasing to be grave. He has never been seen to laugh, but often to weep. His figure is slender and erect; his hands and arms are beautiful to see. His conversation is serious, sparing and modest. He is the fairest of the children of men.

There are those who go the length of believing that this is nothing less than the police description of Jesus at the time of his arrest. But it is quite certain that the *Letter of Lentulus* is a forgery, although even then it is not impossible that it does embody a genuine tradition. It may be that we have to say of the appearance of Jesus, with Augustine, 'We are utterly ignorant.' But this we can say, that in the silent years in Nazareth Jesus was building up the physical manhood without which he could not have faced or completed his task.

Throughout the silent years Jesus was learning the meaning of family life. The name for God which came most naturally to the lips of

Jesus was Father; and the very use of that word is itself a very beautiful compliment to Joseph. It was said of Martin Luther that he hesitated to pray the Lord's Prayer and to say 'Our Father', because his own father had been so stern, so unbending, so unsympathetic that the word 'father' was not a word which he loved. To Jesus the name 'father' was the most natural and the most precious name for God, and it was in the home at Nazareth that he must have learned the meaning of that word.

There were words which Jesus heard in the home in Nazareth which lingered in his mind all his days. Once he came to a little girl whom all others thought to be dead, and said softly: *'Talitha cumi'*, which means, as we might say, 'Little lamb, get up!' (Mark 5.41). Where did Jesus hear a child called 'Little lamb'? Surely these were the words which he had heard the gentle Mary croon over himself and over his brothers and sisters, when they were very young. Throughout the years Jesus was discovering that it was God indeed who had set the solitary in families (Ps. 68.6). He was no monkish ascetic; he grew up within a home.

The work in the shop and the life in the family were both parts of the essential education and preparation of Jesus for his task, for through them his full identity with men was established. In the shop he knew the problem and the anxiety of making a living for a household. He knew the problem of dealing with unreasonable people. He learned to see men at their best and at their worst and as they were. In the home he had to solve the universal problem of living together. Jesus did not live a secluded, isolated, protected life, on which the wind was not allowed to blow. He knew the life of the men whom he had come to save.

Throughout the silent years Jesus learned to love God's world, and to see God in creation and in common things. Jesus grew to manhood in the loveliest part of Palestine. Around the Sea of Galilee there was the Plain of Gennesareth, and the Jews sometimes said that the word Gennesareth meant Prince of Gardens. They called that plain 'the unequalled garden of God'. They called the countryside around Sepphoris 'a land flowing with milk and honey'. There was a Jewish proverbial saying that it was easier to raise a legion of olive trees in

Galilee than to bring up one child in the rest of Palestine. Merrill in his book on Galilee lists the trees which grew there in the time of Jesus—the vine, the olive, the fig, the oak, the walnut, the terebinth, the palm, the cedar, the cypress, the balsam, the fir-tree, the pine, the sycomore, the bay-tree, the myrtle, the almond, the pomegranate, the citron, the oleander. In Galilee, said Josephus, trees which would not grow together elsewhere grew in the same place, as if nature were doing violence to herself.

It was in this land of loveliness that Jesus grew up. He learned to love the sight of the sower sowing his seed (Matt. 13.1-8); of the corn field ripening steadily under God's sun (Mark 4.26-29); of the mustard bush with the birds clustering round to steal the little black seeds (Mark 4.30-32); of the scarlet poppies and anemones blooming their one day on the hillside in raiment such as Solomon in his glory never wore (Matt. 6.28,29). Throughout the years Jesus was learning to look on the world as 'the garment of the living God'.

He was learning to use the common actions and happenings of life as windows through which to catch a glimpse of the truth and the glory of God. He watched his mother Mary using the leaven when she baked the bread (Matt. 13.33). He marked the frenzied search when a woman lost a silver coin amidst the rushes on the cottage floor (Luke 15.8f.). He knew what happened when one carelessly put new wine into old bottles whose skins had lost their elasticity, and how a new patch on an old garment could leave things worse than ever (Matt. 9.16f.). He knew the joy of a village wedding feast (Matt. 9.15); he watched the fishermen with their nets (Matt. 13.47); he was moved by the care of the shepherd for his sheep (Luke 15.4-6). He watched the children playing at weddings and funerals in the village street (Matt. 11.16f.).

Few great teachers have had their feet so firmly planted on the ground as Jesus had. In these early years he was learning every day how to get from 'the here and now' to the 'there and then'. He was learning how near eternity is to time, and how to see God in the life and actions and the things of every day.

Throughout the silent years Jesus was learning to dream. Nazareth itself is tucked away in a hollow of the hills, a secluded little town. But the extraordinary thing about Nazareth was that the world passed almost by its door. It has been said that Judaea was on the way to nowhere and Galilee was on the way to everywhere, for the great roads of the East passed through Galilee. Jesus had only to climb the hilltop above the cup-like hollow of Nazareth and the passing world was at his feet. From there he could look down on the great Road of the Sea, the road which went from Damascus to Egypt, one of the greatest highways in the world with its merchantmen and its caravans. From there he could see the strategic Road of the East which went out from the Mediterranean coast to Parthia and to the eastern bounds of the Roman Empire with its Arab traders and its Roman legions clanking on their way. From there, if he looked westwards, he could see the blue waters of the Mediterranean, with the sails of the ships and the cargoes of those who do business in great waters.

So Jesus could climb the hilltop behind Nazareth, and from there he could see the roads coming and going to the ends of the earth. It was there that he must have dreamed his dreams, and it may be that it was there that something first said to him: 'I, when I am lifted up from the earth, will draw all men to myself' (John 12.32).

It was in the silent years that Jesus learned to pray. When he went out upon his task, it was his custom to take everything to God; again and again he withdrew from men to be alone with God. When he was in his last agony on the Cross, he prayed: 'Father, into thy hands I commit my spirit' (Luke 23.46). That is a quotation from Ps. 31.5 with the one word 'Father' added. But more, that was the first prayer which every Jewish mother taught her child to say, when he lay down to sleep at night, before the dark came down. It was with a prayer that he had learned at Nazareth on his lips that Jesus ended his agony and finished his task.

One thing more is to be added. Eighteen years is a long time to wait, and it may be that there was a very special reason for that delay. After the story of the birth of Jesus Joseph vanishes from the narrative. Even as early as the marriage feast at Cana of Galilee there is no word of Joseph being there (John 2.1-11). By far the most likely explanation is that Joseph was dead, and that the young Jesus had to take upon his shoulders the family business and the support of his mother Mary and of his younger brothers and sisters (Mark 6.3), and that he had to stay in Nazareth until there was some one in the family old enough to take over the carpenter's shop and to earn a living for the family. The day was to come when Jesus was to tell a story about a servant who because he had been faithful in a few things was made master over many things (Matt. 25.21-23). In that story Jesus was telling his own story, for it is quite certain that, if Jesus had not been faithful in the simple and the elementary duties of the home, God could never have given him the task of being the Saviour of the world. Throughout the silent years Jesus was learning many things; and in the performance of the simple duties he was proving himself for the task which God was to give him to do.

Let no man despise the simple duties of the home and the tasks which lie to his hand, for therein, for him as for Jesus, there is the purpose of God. Rabindranath Tagore, the Indian mystic, has a poem:

> At midnight the would-be ascetic announced: 'This is the time to give up my home and seek for God. Ah, who has held me so long in delusion here?' God whispered, 'I', but the ears of the man were stopped. With a baby asleep at her breast lay his wife, peacefully sleeping on one side of the bed. The man said, 'Who are ye that have fooled me so long?' The voice said again: 'They are God,' but he heard it not. The baby cried out in his dream, nestling closer to his mother. God commanded: 'Stop, fool; leave not thy home,' but he heard not. God sighed and complained: 'Why does my servant wander to seek me, forsaking me?'

The Son of God, when he came into this world, prepared himself to save the world by serving in a home.

INDEX